BREAKING FREE

Matthew,
Hope you enjoy the book!!

Matthew.

Hope you enjoy the book !!

BREAKING FREE

MATT SWAIN

NEW DEGREE PRESS

BREAKING FREE

ISBN   979-8-88504-584-1 *Paperback*
            979-8-88504-929-0 *Kindle Ebook*
            979-8-88504-818-7 *Ebook*

Dedication:

To my past, present and future self.

Contents

"The ultimate way you and I get lucky is if you have some success early in life, you get to find out early it doesn't mean anything."

—DAVID FOSTER WALLACE

Author's Note

I knew my experiences were trying to teach me something. I realized I had to explore them in a book to find out exactly what. I found the answer. Here is that book.

Preface

"You only live once, but if you do it right, once is enough."

—MAE WEST

It takes a lot to walk away from your dream life. Chasing money and success was all I ever really knew. I wasn't sure if I could be anything different or if I could change. After all, I had worked so hard to achieve my dream, conquer the doubts, and create the magical imaginations I once visualized. But I felt empty. The whole culture told me to keep climbing, chasing, and striving further up the ladder and soon the approval, satisfaction, and happiness I longed for would arrive. But that day never came.

I began to question whether my ideas about my dream life, with the endless money, fast cars, and glamorous helicopters, were actually my own. And whether the logic of the culture transformed into the peace and happiness I was seeking. Looking back, it's clear my inner voice whispering deep within battled with the forces that were thrust upon me. I found my heart telling me to be who I really was. I sadly had to become so utterly lost, mentally broken, exhausted, and hit rock bottom, before I finally listened.

My dream life had actually become a trap full of everything I had ever wanted. I was living the dream. But I became imprisoned. Destroyed by the very things I wanted, as they were not, in fact, what I truly wanted but what I had been conditioned to desire. I had mentally attempted to open the door. I had tried so hard to kick down the exit, to use all my weight and force to get out. But I've now realized the room was not in fact locked; the handle just opened when I finally allowed myself to be who I was.

This realization, that I could live the life I wanted to, has changed my whole perspective. And it can change yours too. But even then, when I understood I could turn the handle, I had to resist the temptation to fit in, overcome the toxic messaging that radiates in today's culture, and carve my own path. I had to diligently follow my heart when the world was telling me to do the opposite. I had to trust who I was even when I didn't want to.

It was a difficult, sometimes painful, hard-hitting journey, but it liberated me to see the truth. To discover my own mind. To become who I really am.

* * *

I was just fourteen when it happened. One autumn afternoon, my parents received a call that I wouldn't be home until later that evening. I was going to be kept behind in detention for my bad behavior. As the minutes passed, I was left in agonizing pain as I knew that I would soon have to return home, walk through the front door, and be met with the shame and humiliation for my actions.

I forcefully dragged one foot in front of the other, walking home at dusk, edging closer to my fate. It felt like the world was crushing me with each step I took. I knew I was going to be in trouble, and I hated myself for it.

I wasn't the popular one in the playground. The good-looking one around all the girls. I wasn't sporty. And now I wasn't clever or well-behaved. As the clock ticked in the classroom after school that day, the amount of evidence showing that I was a worthless loser had peaked. Crying in my room that night, I arrived at the conclusion: I wasn't enough.

Instead of being told I was okay, that I was accepted for my mistakes and lack of abilities, I was told the complete opposite. I felt I was a failure. It was made clear to me that I wasn't a good child. That everyone expected me to be more and to be better. That I had let everyone down. This, coupled with a series of similar events, made it clear no one believed in me, nor had hopes of me living a life full of opportunity and prospects. I was invisible to everyone.

I would embark on a journey to change that.

So in my room that evening I created a mask out of necessity. I carefully constructed a character. One I would play. A fabricated version of myself focused on the pursuit of success, achievements, and greatness, that would end up becoming me. Designed to protect me from feeling the inadequacies I had developed inside. To hide the real me, the failure, underneath a heroic performer.

I would perfect, strive, chase, climb and conquer. I would win medals, battle demons, and triumph over obstacles. I would stand on the podium and be celebrated for my abilities. I would bathe in the approval and validation of others. Most importantly, I would become rich and successful. *No doubt about that.*

I would show my classmates, parents, teachers, friends, aunts and uncles, the postman, everyone who I ever laid eyes on that I was great. That they should never have doubted me. That they were wrong. And I was right.

* * *

This characterized version of myself took me on an epic ride, full of driving ambition, worldly success, and accomplishments. From major client deals to business class-travel, exotic locations, unbelievable amounts of money and glamorous parties. But a ride that also led me down a road of misguided beliefs, tragic mistakes, and wrong turns.

I also journeyed into a new state of awareness that allowed me to experience profound realizations. I discovered that I needed to escape the idea that I wasn't enough and learn my own worth. I had to run away from the constant pleasing, performing, and perfection I was striving for and set my own boundaries. I had to shake off the cultural dogma and societal programming that prevented me from being myself and find the liberating freedom which comes from fully expressing yourself. Stay clear from doing the 'right' thing so I didn't end up living someone else's life. I had to loosen the chains my mind had become enslaved to and define my own truth.

I had to break free.

CHAPTER 1:

The Shiny Building of My Dreams

"I think everybody should get rich and famous and have everything they ever dreamed of, so they can see that it's not the answer."

—JIM CARREY

The building stood tall, reaching into the wispy clouds, slowly grouping in the sky while my eyes glistened in amazement as the reflections from the huge, towering, shining panels of glass stretched effortlessly toward dizzying heights. I wasn't fazed by the enormity of my surroundings. In fact, quite the opposite. The building represented what I had been working toward. I believed that the scale of the skyscraper was in some ways representative of my personal achievement. I concluded that I had achieved extraordinary things by being here. That I deserved this. This was who I was and what I wanted to become.

This was the shiny building of my dreams. As I stared straight ahead, I was stunned that I had actually made it happen. That I had turned my wildest imaginations into reality. The faint memories that formulated in my mind years ago, visualizing what I wanted my future to hold, had crystallized into the real world right in front of my eyes. After years of aspiring to stand in this very spot, here I was.

I overcame the odds, transformed doubt into destiny, converted struggle into victory. I had heroically battled away those who didn't believe in my talents, abilities, and potential. Blocked out the whispers that took place behind my back that attempted to infiltrate my mind and vision. Ignored those who didn't believe that a life full of achievements, success, and money was a happy one. At eighteen years old, I was living my dream. It felt like I had conquered the world and I was staring at the prize.

I felt my heart rise and fall, pulsing with excitement, the oxygen traveling around my body. I let out a deep exhale. Success felt so good. I fixated my eyes on the glass revolving door now just meters in front of me. Momentarily, the rest of the world stopped. The busyness around me, the movements of others, and the motion of the city faded from my sight. I was being drawn in like a vortex, a spotlight placed above me watching my every move.

My body felt the significance of this moment, the realization that I had made it. I edged closer, felt the rush of air from the spinning doors ahead. Money, success, power, achievement, and status oozed through an open gap in the entrance and slowly flooded down the marble steps to my feet. My ego absorbed every part of this feeling that it could. Savoring the moment and collecting the reward it had wanted for so long.

My mask bathed in the glory of what it had accomplished. My character was a success. *I've made it.*

I convinced myself that this was the mountaintop I should climb toward. The very atmosphere was filled with an unwavering sense that a career-focused, money-orientated life was an admirable pursuit. And I was in the heart of the world of high finance and business. In the center of a city dedicated to chasing and winning.

London's main objective was creating the most glamorous, modernistic towers where the race to the top would take place. A contest founded upon the principle of climbing quickly and relentlessly. A competition in which heights, appearance, and prestige indicated your worth. Although an untold, silent truth, it was clear to me that everyone was a participant, desperately contending with each other. It never occurred to me where the desire to compete originated, the purpose behind, it or even where the end point was. The finish line had long been a well-guarded secret. But all that mattered was the inner desire to win and succeed. It was an inherent force deep within. An instinct. To appear prestigious. To climb the ladder. To conquer barriers. To soak up success.

Success was a continually defining characteristic. Woven carefully underneath the streets, tangling its way through the winding rivers, under the historic monuments, between the narrow high-rise flats where people hung washing on small balconies and struggled to keep up with the changing city. Success was the driving force for life. Despite the traditions and centuries-old foundations on which the physical world lay, within our minds, there was a powerful awakening of a new desire. An ambition in the ascent. The days of merely doing your job, paying the bills and being part of a community had almost all but disappeared. And what developed was a dream. A dream that became my own. A dream I longed for. A dream I would live.

I'm going to climb to the top. Soak in success. Drive the fastest cars. Holiday on the biggest yachts. Have the biggest bank account.

The strength of this idea that was ever present in my environment permeated my own mind. Quickly becoming the center of my attention. I too had become gladly entangled with this deep sense of desire, this idea of battling to crazy heights. I had been sucked into the commercial messaging, the worship of work as a moral virtue, the propagandizing pressuring me to be more; it was pulling me in like a gravitational force.

I stared and looked at the impressive tower ahead, knowing that I was working at a world-renowned, prestigious, corporate firm with the glass box, pivotal meetings, and earning potential. But deep down I knew I actually desired the feeling I thought achieving this goal would bring. The satisfaction in achieving milestones beyond the expectations of others. The power I would be trusted with as a result of where I worked. The approval that I meant something to the world.

I was desperate to experience that feeling of success that my mask yearned for. For so long, the glare on the shining glass windows had prevented me from seeing inside, from fully belonging, from savoring the deep satisfaction from everything I had worked toward. Until now.

I was finally one of them.

I moved through the soaring entrance, past the guarded gates keeping the rest of the world outside, into the office foyer which was like stepping inside a beautiful palace. My wooden heels clicked and glided across the sheer expansiveness and scale of the place I could now call home. I was cocooned from the outside world. The glare now blocked out the rest of London. I had won the race. But another was just about to start.

My goals and desires would soon become moving targets, an elusive cloud that I would struggle to grasp. But for now, I let my body adjust to this long-awaited reality and let my eyes absorb the significance of this moment. Because, I knew deep down, that the intensity and power of this feeling would forever remain a distinct and consequential marker on my journey. That this moment would define me.

The glitz and glamour continued to reveal itself like a magic show as I explored deeper into the building. Large, white conference tables were arranged as I joined the other new starters who were a part of my cohort, all dressed in an array of well-tailored suits and crisp shirts with their neat collars freshly pressed. Our faces were etched with eagerness in anticipation of the years ahead as we discussed what this day and the future meant. I was obsessed with the fact that I was being accelerated. I was on the fast-track scheme to the top. On track to gain a top degree coupled with world-class experience. One of a handful of selected individuals. This was exactly what I wanted—the quickest route to the top. I wanted to win the race. This was how I was going to do it.

I bypassed the traditional route in going to a university, gaining internships, and getting a degree before starting. I was beginning in the deep end. All in order for me to advance and progress my way up the ladder even quicker so I could obtain maximum status. I desperately wanted the fastest development, the most opportunities, and was hungry for anything that would increase my chances to beat the rest of the world to what I saw as my rightful place.

I purposefully discounted the fact that I may have become swept up alongside the clever marketing and generous perks that were plastered all over career brochures that laid scattered wherever my head turned. That the reason I may have chosen this was for the handsome salary and the fact that I would be working in close contact with the smartest and hardest working people. A career that would open doors, give me the skills I needed to succeed, and where I would receive nods of approval wherever I walked.

I had romanticized about this career path, seeking this highly competitive scheme which on the surface offered everything an ambitious young student like myself could aspire to. But underneath there was a deep pull in wanting the challenge and status of working somewhere where so few got accepted; exclusivity was the secretly motivating factor why this route seemed so appealing.

As I made my way to the welcome reception drinks on the top floor of the building, I couldn't help but fall in love with the view. I stared across the vast city, overlooking the rooftops around me. Admiring from the heights I looked up to just weeks before.

The large reception room on the twentieth floor was a hive for activity. Executive partners, directors from huge multinational businesses and the very best in the firm were dressed in their finest suits and meandered with their tall, thin glass flutes filled with champagne. I had brief encounters with them, although they didn't realize that they were only greeting my carefully placed, invisible mask. The fictional version of me, that now incorporated and absorbed the behavior, attitudes, and ideas of those around me into the character I played.

I was oblivious to the apparent importance of the event, distracted from our chairman proudly sharing the values of the firm. Instead, I stood by one of the towering glass panels stretching far above me. I saw straight past the glass, without a reflection or glare preventing me from seeing clearly. I was able to gaze and dream into the distance.

It wasn't just the physical distance between the ground and my newly found heights. But the symbolism behind what the gap created. What the separation stood for. Feeling so unreachable, as if I was on top of the world. Shielded and out of reach from everyone else. I never wanted to be on the outside trying to look in again. *I felt safe at last.*

This was now normal. This was now my life. The feeling of success was now a permanent reality. Newness swarmed all these experiences and I struggled to fully comprehend how I had managed to make it. How the little boy who had a dream somehow made it happen. How I had managed to transition into the glossy world that was now my home.

I slowly entered the lift to return back to the ground, transporting me back into the outside world. As the doors slid shut, I was suddenly struck with a momentary feeling of loneliness as I realized that the possibility of living in this world of glitz and glamour, money, and success at all times, might be a difficult task.

* * *

The early days continued to be an exhilarating, fast-learning environment. But as the weeks passed, the routine and regularity started to set in. The rhythm and pace of life with its initial anticipation and excitement slowed and alongside it, the meaning, purpose, and success faded too. I hid the fact that the majority of my days were spent staring behind complicated spreadsheets and trapped in four white walls.

However, I still soaked in the enormous pleasure from being within the grandeur of executive board rooms. From the glamor of being instrumental in significant client meetings. I kept moving and pushing and climbing. To the next client. The next challenge. But I couldn't avoid my own internal suspicion that underlying all these feelings was a strong sense of self-importance that comforted me wherever I walked. It was like a red carpet beneath my feet. A soothing mark of validation for my whole body.

Each morning I jumped in my brand-new luxury car, feeling my hands run over the smooth leather steering wheel, the stereos pumping my veins with energy, my foot pressed harshly on the accelerator followed by an emotion of power that consumed me, as the exhausts revved loudly, marking my arrival and departure. I let the wind rush through my hair. I was happy and it felt like I owned the world. I now had a physical representation of my mind's work. A symbol for my success.

But as I became accustomed to my new life, I realized that the feelings I so greatly desired were temporary in nature. My character always felt a feeling of immense approval. But deep inside it was followed by an eerie emptiness.

Nonetheless, my characterized self adored the status I received from discussions around where I worked. Everyone desperately idolized my job and I let them. I was perceived to be in possession of desired human characteristics, such as ambition and power, from the busyness that radiated from my life. I came to realize that my worth as a person was largely driven from the allure of my job, especially at my age. My choices were constantly validated, and I felt a sense of belonging as I instantly gained attention and interest from my accomplishments. But it never made me feel whole as a person and I always departed those conversations with a fading sense of happiness.

Yet, I had become so convinced in the desire to compete in the race and concluded I would be required to chase, conquer, and climb even more. I had to maintain success to feed my mask and disguise the failure within.

* * *

My early observations saw a world full of everybody hustling for money, desiring status, and working obsessively. Yet, my eyes also saw the mundanity, boredom, and pain that it appeared other people experienced. In order to obtain happiness, I presumed I needed to aim higher. Go one step further.

I was sure that my ideas and conclusions about life were right. That my outlook was not a mirage. That achieving on a bigger, more dramatic scale, at elevated heights, would lead to the life I truly wanted. And that embodied what it took. That I could attain greatness.

I wasn't going to stop when I could do more. Push harder. Be better. My blood flowed with endless potential. It was my nitrogen fuel. My hidden power. It was my everything. And I was going to see where it could take me. See how many mountains I could climb. How many achievements I could conquer. How many things I could be.

CHAPTER 2:

A Different World

"We seldom realize, for example, that our most private thoughts and emotions are not actually our own. For what we think in terms of languages and images we did not invent but which were given to us by our society."

—ALAN WATTS

It was pitch black. Our windowless hotel room was dark. A faint humming from a multitude of car horns bled through the walls, a subtle hint as to what was outside the four walls. My body slowly adjusted, waking from its sleep, and the warm electric feeling of being somewhere new arose from within me.

The wheels of the Boeing 777 screeched down at New Delhi airport in the early hours of the morning, meaning that the journey to our hotel was under the cover of darkness and so the experience of India remained undiscovered.

As I stretched, shaking off the short night's sleep, I was eager to see beyond our room. As I slowly moved down the solid steps to the main door, the sound from outside got louder and more intense. As I edged closer, the door was ajar and there was a deep magnetic pull that drew me in.

The doors thin opening allowed light to stream through that pushed me forward with force. It felt like I had discovered a magical kingdom behind a secret opening. As if I had uncovered a whole new dimension to the world. A force with so much power, so much presence, I wondered whether it could be real.

My eyes slowly adjusted to the radiating light from the sun: extreme, yet dancing, in the sky. I took a deep breath and just stood there, not quite believing my eyes.

Tuk Tuks darted from all angles as if they had a mind of their own. Small stalls that sold all manners of food lined the streets in a completely unorderly fashion. Signposts littered the buildings on either side. Carts maneuvered around the frantic movements of people, small delivery trucks, and cows that roamed freely. Traffic churned through the streets with wondrous and mysterious efficiency—a ballistic dance of buses, trucks, bicycles, cars, oxcarts, and scooters.

As my eyes widened, the magic of the city continued to amaze. I surrendered to its beauty. It was wild and exciting. Old romantic buildings stood side by side. Neglected remnants of old structures haphazardly crumbled. While on either side of the road, lavish displays of market vegetables and silks were displayed. A cacophony of music played from the moving taxis and store fronts. Millions of supernatural colors surrounded me. The fragrances that hovered around me were all-encompassing. And there were more smiles in the eyes on those crowded streets than in any other place I'd ever known.

I stepped into the moving scene. The magic and energy kept pulling me closer, step-by-step moving forward into the moving scene, getting closer to the beating heart of India.

Keen to explore more of this magical city, I jumped in a Tuk Tuk for a short ride around the local markets. My jaw was endlessly dropped in amazement coupled with shock at the sights of chickens running around shops, walls that looked like they would topple, and near crashes with other vehicles. The Tuk Tuk darted around the corridor-like market lanes while I was thrown around in the back seat, trying to look around while also trying to hold on tight. The whole experience felt like I was on a ride; theatrical and surreal. But while for me, it was an entertaining ride, to everyone in India it was their normal life.

I was so far removed from what I knew. I couldn't believe it. It felt like a different world.

As we travelled through parts of New Delhi, Agra, and Jaipur, wherever I looked, I had the same fascination with the sheer contrast to my life back home in the concrete city. Around every corner and with every person provided an inspiring insight into a whole different life. An existence unknown to me before this. But I couldn't help but suspect whether it was genuine. I couldn't grasp why they weren't striving for the pursuit of more. Why they weren't participating in the same race.

Travelling the long distances between the beautiful cities, we stopped along the way at roadside cafes. Dusty lay-bys were turned into places to sit and buy snacks. On uncomfortable plastic chairs, we sat watching the cars whizz past. Litter surrounded us and everything was a cluttered mess. It felt like a strange place to be.

Every little thing mattered in London. From the pristine presentation of the pavements, the place I brought my morning coffee from, the precise minute I turned up for work to the style of shirt I wore to drink receptions. The ideas were cocooned to London and were nowhere to be seen here. India was instead all about simplicity. There was a focus on what's really important in life, that slowly revealed itself to me like a curtain veil slowly opening.

This trip expanded and detonated my imagination. Every person we came across seemed like a new and fascinating character, every destination was a dreamland. But at the same time, their happiness seemed naïve and delusional. There was no mountaintop here. No place to reach toward. *How could you be happy when you could chase more?*

The pace of life was unhurried and leisurely, as people moved between market stalls, tended to roaming animals, or sipped a cup of hot tea. But there was a real sense of purpose that I hadn't seen up close before. I observed life unfold in that moment, in that one place in the middle of a huge country, part of a gigantic Earth. Yet, my mindset conflicted with the innate gracefulness of India. *I had places to be.*

I stood and stared at a young boy, a similar age to myself, sat cross-legged amongst the chaos of the surroundings, take a deep breath, close his eyes and sit completely still in peace. My eyes locking in on his calmness. I couldn't imagine being able to sit still. I was used to being in the race. Running for the next goal. I wasn't ready to laze around when there were opportunities in front of me to chase.

There was a sense that India felt so exhilaratingly free. The spirit of India was unconfined. It was a place of liberty without constraints. Monkeys roamed freely, and carefully wandered on the narrow rooftops, along precarious wires and weaved in and around the busy streets. There was a strong aura of acceptance. Freedom was innate in India. A first principle. I wandered freely here too and moved as I pleased. But London was a place of conformity. Competing upward. I had been conditioned with one destiny. But here it seemed like you carved your own. *Obviously, I couldn't have done anything as radical as this.*

While they couldn't purchase flashy cars and well-tailored suits, they could meander with their time. They had no desire for maximizing their opportunities and optimizing their performance, as I sought. I believed was superior. As much as their freedom seemed appealing, I couldn't help but wonder why they didn't have dreams to chase and ambitions to conquer.

People walked with peace and purpose, no matter how little materially they had. I observed how they never asked for anything. They never complained. There was an unshakable and profound sense that everyone was content, despite them not living the life of glossy luxury I had created. While I lived in a permanent state of perpetual chasing, they were grateful for what they had. I believed that happiness was a state achieved through accomplishments and possessions. *Were they happy at all then?*

I was blissfully unaware at the time that my freedom would be dependent on my willingness to accept the truth and finally listen to myself in the same way that India was a country based upon the foundation of openness and honesty. But for now, I was still racing. Gaining any advantage I could. My mindset whirring with what I could become.

I walked the streets feeling a disconnection between my mind and where I was physically. I felt unnerved by the density of purposes and intensity. I was left puzzled with ideology that was a million miles from the beliefs that usually surrounded me. Confused at their attitude and approach to life. It was as if I had walked on stage and found myself in a performance of some extravagant, complex show and I didn't have a script.

India's culture was strong and powerful, and I was absorbed in the bizarre craziness of daily life. But as much as I was stunned, my mind remained clear on my own personal objectives in life. The money, power, and status. I was too self-assured and confident in my philosophy and this righteousness solidified with the more I saw. My mindset simply strengthened.

My mask remained securely fitted. My character knew what was required from me. That success and money would continue to drive and propel me forward in order to achieve my life's pursuits. The freedom in India seemed so distant, like a faraway galaxy, a tease, an impossible hazy dream. I was here on Earth to strive. These people wouldn't attain the goals I would achieve. They didn't have the wild aspirations I was chasing. They would never have what I did.

The race controlled my every move and thought. The competition that was taking place in London was my true calling. None of what I saw in India was going to help me in my pursuit. The path of glory I was paving was the better choice. The right direction. India didn't have the recipe to win. They weren't going to get to the finish line like I would.

There was no way to win here.

My time in India was the polar opposite to the world of high finance I knew so well. The dull boardrooms were swapped for a bizarre hive of activity and an array of fascinating colors. But India didn't change my mind. But it left a mark, a vague trace of a different life with a new perspective. Deep inside my mind, a pattern of neurons had connected. So submerged under years of conditioning I wouldn't notice. But the subtle shift was there. Etched into my inner memory.

* * *

Arriving at London Heathrow Airport, I was greeted with a cloudy, drizzling January morning. Life returned to normality for me, and I felt a draining sense, leaving the excitement behind. My head pressed against the window of the car to go home. Grayness polluted the air. As the miles of monotonous motorway flew by, with the central reservation whizzing past, and the orderly white lanes in the neat lines. I couldn't help but long to be somewhere else.

But I was now back in the world where I could pursue my version of happiness. The right way. I had my goals and objectives back in sight. Ambition filled the air once again. I took deep breaths, inhaling the aspiration. My visit to India had been a temporary shock to the system. There was a fading feeling that something was missing from my fast-lane London life. But the glossy skyscrapers, sharp suits, and extravagance soon diminished the idea that India may have been trying to teach me a lesson.

My mind circled as I settled back into life and work. But the general aura of India remained as a feeling inside of me. An amazing glimpse at another side of life, one that I didn't know existed. One that seemed to provide a beautiful life. But they had something far different to what I thought I wanted.

CHAPTER 3:

Who Made the Choice

"Sometimes it's the smallest decisions that can change your life forever."

—KERI RUSSELL

The sun was low in the sky. I was away from the glaring lights of the city. Even as a child, I could sense that the rhythm of daily life had disappeared. Those evenings, as the sun slowly departed from sight, with the windless air and radiating warmth, were pure bliss. I ran around the park, playing football long into those summers' evenings, small droplets of sweat appearing around my cheeks, and grass stains on my t-shirt and socks.

There was no place I needed to be. No task that needed completing. No expectations on my future. As my feet ran across the grass, I was so free, I could have run for miles. I was so happy. *Nothing to chase. I could just be me.*

I was hopeful that maybe one day I would return to this state of mind. Return to the peace in those evenings where I could be whoever I wanted. Reclaim that freedom that I lost to my future. I had no responsibilities. The world expected nothing from me. No one wanted me to change the world or become a millionaire. Not even myself.

But everything would soon become different, and I was never going to be able to return to the innocent bliss I was once protected by. I couldn't turn back the clocks to re-experience those moments where I was the freest man on Earth. Just a boy. Just a normal boy.

As a child I would smile aimlessly at the simple passing of daily life, be so excited with the idea of waking up to a new day, it felt like I could dance with all the freedom I had. Not just in what I could do, but how I could think. I was free to imagine. To dream. I longed to travel and see the world. To be a part of something bigger than myself. But this too slowly disappeared as I grew into the culture that told me to follow an identical, singular line. A path so narrow it felt like I could fall off.

* * *

There was a constant and consistent drawn-out narrative that replayed many times during the course of my childhood. It didn't seem to matter the time of day, the environment, or who was around me; there was one thing I was always asked. It was from the accumulation of these moments. The sheer quantity of them that changed my view on the world. Which started to change how I viewed myself.

The cream-colored paint was slowly breaking on the walls, evident in the corners, just above the circling heating pipes.

The room was bare and uninspiring but as I sat on a well-made plastic chair, I noticed the high ceilings which, in ways, were irrelevant. Maybe it was a sign I always had my heights set on the top. It was too early to tell. The sun beamed in through the large, glass windows that ran down one side. A whiteboard lay centrally focused in the room, hung with care. Which, everyone else in the class also stared directly toward.

Teachers paced in front of the class, as if a magic maestro was commanding the stage. They glared with fascination into our eyes, wishing for us to use our metaphorical crystal balls to determine our futures. I always answered comically, relaxed and oblivious. But underneath, deep below what I could comprehend, tucked under the surface, my mind was being changed.

It seemed impossible for such few words to command such a deep action. But nonetheless as I grew with the days, the cuts became more permanent, and my mind started to notice the strength of these messages.

There never seemed any bad intention, no purpose, no meaning behind the specific messages that were projected onto me. I would daydream for hours out the windows, as if beautifully unaware of the future, carelessly thinking about wherever my mind wandered. It appeared to have ignored me in some ways, but nonetheless the marks were there.

It became clear, from the classroom, to playgrounds, to after-school play dates to my own family dinner table, that the most important question for me to answer was: What did I want to be when I grew up?

This would be the pursuit that would absorb my sole focus. Looking back, it's hard to imagine how pivotal those remarks were. On the surface they seem so harmless. Adults wanting to peek inside my whirring processor, I guess, to protect me, to make sure I was on a stable route, to make sure my ideas were realistic.

But how could I know what I wanted to be? Why did I have to be something? What did growing up even mean? I pushed these internal ideas to one side and answered with all my freedom with the first thought that came to mind. Over the years, I had wanted to be so many things. Yet that question remained. Until I decided that getting the best possible answer would be my life's sole mission. My heart's only objective.

This was the deep cut, that somehow got lodged in my waking mind. It may be the spark that formed the driving force that led me to where I am today. But it also created the deep-rooted insecurity that caused me pain beyond those around me would have wished. The classroom that day seemed so distant in the past, yet it started the change that catalyzed my life. Shifted my direction.

* * *

With college exams on the horizon and the choices that would need to be made, I was running out of time before I would play out my response. That I would choose a career. A direction. But as time progressed, the roads ahead narrowed, and my own freedom waned. The road in front began to form and take shape ahead of me. Becoming ever more fixated. Its roots digging ever deeper. My own life, which

I thought I had agency and control over was being mapped with fine ink in front of me. Externalities dictated so much of my surroundings that I started to forget whether my grand, extravagant plans were of my own making.

Everyone had the dream of me following the standard societal blueprint. The well-trodden path of taking a great university placement, followed by a high flying corporate role where I would achieve and succeed, eventually owning a home, having fancy holidays, a healthy bank balance, and everything in between. The modern dream maybe.

The subtle formation of expectations built around me like walls surrounding what I could achieve, both inside the classroom with my end of year exams and outside in the world.

This belief in what I should achieve came to change the entire trajectory of my life. Overnight the identity of a hard worker, exam-focused, ambitious student became synonymous with me. Teachers liken this to my inner nature, my essential being. My family members say it's my philosophy, my religion.

They predict it's going to be my epitaph.

I longed to be seen for who I was, but I was just a façade of achievement which was celebrated among teachers, peers, and family. So much of my identity had been connected with being a high achiever. Straight As. Awards. Leadership programs. My mask was happy that it was being acknowledged and rewarded for its work. But there was never ever any breathing room for me to show up any differently than the expectations projected onto me.

My life had become swept up like the wind behind these ideas but whenever I seemed to grasp them, my hands would move through air and the ideas would vanish in front of my very eyes. I never realized that I had lost control over my own mind.

But whenever I caught glimpses of the world I was told to head into, the world I was told I should want, the world I felt compelled toward, it seemed so right. I was so sure it could offer everything I wanted. It seemed to make so much sense.

I attended "insight days," where I explored the opportunities available, spoke to existing employees, and met with an array of senior figures at large corporate firms. I honed in on my interview practice and prepared a winning CV. I buzzed with excitement from the taste of the world I would be entering and was hungry for more. There was an attractive force that dragged me forward onto the pedestal that lay ahead. That I was desperate to climb onto. It was impossible to resist. It became the center of my life. The critical driver of everything.

I was both naive and confident. Naive because I had no real idea of the scale of what I was moving toward. But confident because how could this not be for me? I was ambitious, wanted money, highly motivated by success, and was aiming for the stars. The pinnacle of life. A mountain of money. I was a dragon with my eyes on the pile of gold. And I had found it.

Although, I began to notice that as the desire to succeed grew stronger, the freedom I once felt diminished. Disappeared from my very existence. With my new ideas forming, I thought I needed to be so much. Be rich. Be a millionaire. Be successful.

Those long evenings in the fading summer sun were a distant memory in my past. Still there to reflect on but firmly covered by my new conclusions about where I should head and what I should be doing. Nothing of the pure simplicity and spontaneity that those evenings brought remained in my life. All the life had been sucked out from my days and I was left with the pure pursuit of supposed greatness and success.

The young boy who dreamt, became a young man with strong ambitions. Yet, as I was admired for my impressive imaginations about the lifestyle I would lead with the cars and helicopters, I found myself feeling inadequate, with a heavy burden that I needed to be something. *The fear of failure creeping back.* I stared into the mirror feeling that I should be so much more. I suddenly had something to prove.

So I upped my game and focused on my mission. Activities that were described to me as important, largely my exams, were now my only pursuit. My only focus. Long had the naivety faded from my life and suddenly I had developed high expectations. That I wanted my worth as a person to be acknowledged, admired, and celebrated. That I wanted more.

Pain and greatness became my Yin and Yang. But the affliction is only visible on reflection. While in the pursuit, it appeared that there was only greatness as this was all everyone ever focused on, leading me to believe that I had, in fact, sacrificed nothing. I would however learn that there would be many sacrifices required in order for me to stand on the podium, celebrating with the trophy that was expected from me.

I was simply a body fulfilling a purpose that was carved long before I was born. But why defeat the inevitable? Why resist when the awaited success would soon be at my fingertips? Just over the verge on the hill ahead. My ego kept my desire for money and success on track, blinding me from the possibility for anything different. It was my beating heart that devoured status and kept my inner drive pumping through my bloodstream, as if it was a survival mechanism.

However, I glossed over the truth that this desire for achievements and status arose from a fear of failure deep inside from that moment after school in detention years earlier. It was lodged in my mind at depths I never fully realized. All my results, successes, achievements and attention, the jokes, my smile, were a subtle projection aimed to hide me from feeling that internally I was a failure. *I wasn't enough.*

It would become my mission to hide the failure I felt inside. I was going to be the golden child. It was going to be the performance of a lifetime. And I would never break character. *Not once.*

So I spent all my time carefully curating and crafting an image of perfection. The desire to appear to be a high achieving individual became a deep-rooted hunger that gave me an unavoidable, prolonged sense of unrestful burning from within. This was my forward propulsion, the motivation and power, that kept pushing me. But it was like fire from a dragon's mouth. An out-of-control force. Its strength ready to pounce on my emotions and true feelings.

The image I had created was strong. It was clear there was just one objective. After all, my grades were everything, I was told. And I believed them. After years of hearing their voices, their messages then became my own. I no longer needed the messages from afar. I started to do it all myself. And so my grades became everything to me. My self-worth was no longer based on me, my values, my thoughts, or who I was. It was based on my results and predicated on me achieving my goals.

I became obsessed with emulating the accomplishments I seemed capable of, which was an internal drive, that felt like a competitive advantage in life. But it created a high-stakes game that I was now living. I now had to formulate tactics and strategies. I had to have the winning hand every game. I had to succeed at all costs. And compulsively avoid failure.

Each good outcome reaffirmed this idea, but each time I failed to meet the bar, the internal pain was worse, and the wound deeper. It felt like a crack started to develop in my image. If there was a test where I was average, a poor result, a failed idea, I felt the world looking down on me. But even worse, I felt my own self-worth evaporate. Because I looked down on myself too. But instead of questioning the very nature of these feelings, I hurtled headfirst toward working harder and doing better.

I, of course, was oblivious to the artificially constructed nature of these standards. I perceived them to be written law and therefore not penetrable. But my own internal measure kept being raised higher, my goals became more outrageous, the amount of money I felt I needed to feel complete rose, the job title I desired became more senior, the impact I wanted to have on the world greater and ultimately the desire to achieve more contagious.

* * *

The moment my pen hit the paper on my training contract, signing my name on the inked dotted line, my choice was final. This was it. Now, I needed to prove to everyone I was going to make my dreams a reality. I could tell everyone was eagerly awaiting my choice. The outcome. What I had selected. But more than that, to demonstrate to myself that I could be everything I was told to be.

I wanted to turn heads and create whispers, beat the pressure, and exceed the expectations. The ambitious, pre-determined identity I was labelled with in order for me to fulfill my potential and move in the millionaire direction I had been talking about.

I was off script a little; I knew that going straight into the working world wasn't what my peers had chosen. But I knew I was skipping a steppingstone to the top, jumping ahead of everyone else. The money, success, and status were finally going to be mine. The long wait would be over.

The choice was decided. My future clear-cut. My ideas formed. But I was left wondering whether the decision had actually been mine.

CHAPTER 4:

Temporarily Escaping

"We don't create a fantasy world to escape reality. We create it to be able to stay."

—LYNDA BARRY

The pain kicked in. As my eyes stared into the blurry boxes of a spreadsheet and my fingers aligned on the keyboard, I couldn't help but feel empty. The glamor had been almost entirely muffled and what remained was a sense of pure dread. Routine and realism drained my feelings, and I had my university exams to complete that would give me the professional qualification, degree, and expertise to excel and go further in my career. But they brought another set of difficulties.

The rest of my life was squashed to just my exams and work once again. But strangely, as my client demands and studying overtook my life and became full of stress, mundanity, and difficulty, I received more success and acknowledgment from the outside world. But I couldn't hide the fact that the more lost I became, the more it consumed me. But these voices proclaiming my achievements were my guiding direction. My emotional fuel.

The exam struggles were magnified to a new level from anything I had experienced previously and juggling them while working all hours of the day further amplified the challenge. As I sat on my kitchen table, I scored barely any marks and knew there was a long road ahead if I was going to achieve the scores I needed to remain in the program and keep my job.

Every moment became an opportunity for me to revise in a desperate attempt to boost my grades. It was as if nothing else mattered. As if my life became dependent on my results—an unhealthy addiction.

But I was soon to learn, that everything in life has a price. I was about to pay my high cost for not listening to myself and moving at pace straight ahead with my blinkers in place. The grueling hours commuting, meetings with clients, and being at my desk late into the evening studying, were objectively bad for my body. Pain lingered in my bones and my eyes were hazy from the tiredness. But most of all my head whirred at a hundred miles an hour without any rest and my energy levels were seriously depleted.

But I was so blinded by my ambition to care about my health. To even begin to realize I may have been heading to a bigger problem. My desire to prove my worth to the world fueled me. To prove to myself and everyone else that I was tough, capable, and successful. *I must hide my failure. No matter the cost.*

The longing to be victorious was so strong, despite everything, it felt like it became encased in a hard sediment. Yet, at the same time, there was an unshakable feeling that no matter how successful, no matter how much money, how far I climbed up the ladder, what my grades were, there was a subtle and silent feeling always pulsating at the back of my mind: I would always be a failure.

Sunday nights I would lie awake, counting down the hours until I had to go to work in the morning, tying my chest into a tight knot. My mind whirred through the extensive list of things I had to do the next day, but really didn't want to. The muffled sound of my alarm clock dragged like a subdued knife through my dreamless sleep. I hit snooze for another ten minutes, wanting anything other than to face the day ahead. I was like a zombie, shuffling to my desk each morning. I never felt fully alive. There was a draining feeling that pulled me to the floor, as if my whole body was a weight to existence.

I was well-practiced at the art of numbing my feelings, and stumbled through the day, using distractions to hide the real issues I faced. While infinite scrolling and refreshing my newsfeed temporarily took the edge off and gave me an immediate boost of dopamine, I never accepted the fact I was struggling. I allowed my natural defenses to prevent myself from superficially digging beyond the problem, not daring to go beyond the façade to the deeper issue.

I normalized and blocked out anything that wasn't helping me progress with my exams and lifestyle. But what else could I have done? So, I reluctantly carried on with my outer life, despite feeling an electric buzzing inside of me telling me I needed a change. A constant nagging beneath my skin.

But, in my eyes, there was no alternative. No other option. I couldn't escape the fixed thoughts about career and progression that run so deeply within society, especially at a firm full of ambitious, young professionals. It was always about what's next. What's on the horizon. The desire to do more and move upward was powerful and prominent and I was drawn to embody these values too.

These exams were a key component to continuing forward in my corporate career upon which my whole worth laid. I felt like I could tell no one of the hardships I faced. That maybe, just maybe, I should quit the program. *But then what?* All those years of dreaming, of working, would have been for nothing. Wasted. Evaporated into thin air. I couldn't bare the pain of this. So I kept chasing. I studied harder.

The attainment of my dream became an act of survival. Through the stress, long nights, and struggles, my goals of becoming rich beyond my imagination, climbing the ladder to crazy heights, and finally feeling lasting success saved my life. I saw the materialization of my early imaginations as my only road to happiness. Failure equaled death. My belief was, when I get to the top of this mountain, I will never feel like a failure again, I will never be sad again. Everything worth living for is at the skyscraper summit. And there is nothing I am unwilling to leave or to lose to get there. *Keep chasing.*

Ultimately, I didn't want to admit that I wanted to reject my early imaginations of my magical dream. And I couldn't bear the thought of not reaching my potential. But I had no coping mechanism to deal with these thoughts. The mistake it felt like I had made. Up to this point, I had entirely identified with the achievements and successes. Taking losses so personally filled me with doubt and regret that leaked into every aspect of my life. The failure I believed I was deep down was peeking into sight. I wasn't prepared for this, so I put all my time and energy into doing anything that was required to get me through.

The fire alarm that goes off as a voice in the back of your head when something is wrong or doesn't feel right soon fades the longer it is left to blare. I denied the warning signs and alarm bells, shutting them out and pressing through with my work. Putting in more hours, having less sleep, and pretending everything was okay.

I buried my shortcomings, and rising doubt, under further layers and layers of performance. I adopted a personality that was cheery, upbeat, and positive. I responded to the dissonance of my world by remaining purely constant. I was always smiling. I was always fun and ready to laugh. *Nothing wrong in my world.*

* * *

My head was by now constantly spinning, scheduling, and cramming. It didn't take long before my headaches became continuous and severe. So, I turned to painkillers to ease my life, to escape from the life I was living.

A tiny white pill became my miracle solution. So small but so powerful. But it was what it symbolized. It was medicine for my mind, it was my relaxation technique, it was my supposed answer to all my problems. As the texture touched my lips it was like warm breath refilling me with life. It was my revival.

Momentarily, for those blissful few minutes, it was like the pure joy of ecstasy running vividly through my bloodstream. I was temporarily escaping. I felt my whole body loosen and float away from the struggles that controlled my life. Anything in attempt to loosen their grasp over me. Anything to escape the pain. To once again feel the faint humming of who I was running freely on the football field return.

But every time, the feeling faded to nothing, and I was hit with the reality that my life truly was a life I hated. No pill, nothing could give me the satisfaction I truly wanted. I thought the pills would allow me to escape the pain, to feel relief, so I kept taking them. But I sadly came to the realization that I wasn't chasing the painkillers; I was desperately chasing the feeling of escapism. The taste of freedom.

I lived in total self-imposed isolation, wrestling day and night with the nightmare my life had become and my utter desperation to get out of the death spiral, to be able to breathe again, to not feel the weight of the world crushing me every second of the day. At the same time, however, I kept chasing more. In all my agony, I still had this deep-rooted burning desire to do more work, revise more for my exams, make more money, and gain more power and success.

This was the moment that not only had I become addicted to pills, but I was hooked on gaining the approval of others. I became obsessed with winning. And to ensure I guaranteed and sustained my stream of massive victories, I became addicted to working, grinding, and obsessively pursuing perfection. But the most perpetuating aspect was my need to fill every second of every day, so that it kept me from having to feel.

I was certainly in denial about my addiction, and it took a while for my abuses to fully catch up with me. I was confused as to whether others at work had the same battles or whether I was missing something. I was sure it couldn't just be me. But life carried on. My drug problem was my little secret. No one knew how I was really feeling. So I just kept going.

My lifestyle remained the same and so my relationship with medication became a more integral and persistent part of my daily functioning as I became more dependent on them to work. I kept telling myself the mountaintop was just ahead. That I could keep going, taking the next step. Make it through another day. That soon I would be staring at the peak looking at a wonderful view. On the top of the world. But it never happened.

Everyone always expected me to feel happy and grateful for the situation I was in. My life was full of everything I was told to have. I was living my childhood dream. Proving my worth. Driving a fancy car. On the outside, I was a great success and had achieved everything I thought would make me happy, but I couldn't help but feel like a broken man inside. And I presumed this pain I felt deep inside was for numbing, hiding, and ignoring. I thought when life got hard, it was because I had messed up and gone wrong somewhere. Pain was a weakness to forget about and pretend it didn't exist. But the more I tried to eliminate it from my mind, the more pills and unhappiness followed.

I felt so isolated. No one would understand what it was like, to have your dreams met but feel so empty inside. The surface level life I was living looked perfect. But this was the misery of it all. If I had everything, why was I so unhappy? *No, grit your teeth and get through it. Stand strong. Be a man!*

Each night I stared deeply into the person looking back at me in the mirror. I struggled to recognize myself. I could see the character I played smile, creating a strong outside shell to get me through the battles I faced. But as I peered into my eyes, into the inner workings of my mind, I could see a man who felt like he had failed, who felt like his world was collapsing around him. My inner spark that was being driven into abandonment. I didn't want it to be like this. This wasn't how life was supposed to turn out. My dreams were starting to look more like a nightmare.

Despite seeing my heart become lost, I was never completely gone; I still had my flicker inside that still smoldered. I knew it could return. That essence was always going to be something I could rediscover. Past memories could become present ones.

I returned to the mirror each night, but it was always the same. Feeling a disconnection between what the outside world saw and how I was feeling inside. As if I could see what needed to be done but couldn't bring myself to take the action. Like there was a gem in my pocket that I couldn't touch. Everyone else's desires controlled me like a puppet. I had chains around my mind that tightened their grip with each comment and day I lived this lie. I longed for the day I would feel myself once again. A wishful dream perhaps. An impossible miracle maybe. But possibly one day it would come true.

* * *

Reflecting back, it was no surprise that I had been caught up with the dreams of others. For my whole childhood I was always compared to my peers. Being asked to be so much. I obsessed, copied, and perfected, desperately trying to appease those around me. An unspoken truth was that I should do everything in my power to work my way up the comparison scoreboard. It was embedded in my very actions. I believed it would be impossible for me to be judged on my own merit. I would always be compared to somebody else.

Walking down the stairs the morning after my parents visited friends or were out on a social occasion, I would face a barrage of questions. About why I wasn't doing what my friends were. Why I wasn't happier. It seemed like everyone was a better person than me.

These conversations conditioned me to believe that the whole world was my competition. In order to rise through the ranks, I needed a bigger office, a fancier job title, more friends, more numbers in my phone, a faster car. My friends, neighbors, peers, and classmates all became a threat to my place on the scoreboard. I would compete tirelessly until I got to the top. Race until I crossed the finish line.

I tore myself up about the decisions I had made. Feeling deeply conflicted from within. I had done everything right, I had thought. Done everything I was supposed to do. *How had I ended up here?* These conversations, this internal conflict further boosted my desire to compete, to make more money and climb the ladder and be more successful. I knew that I could be the best. That I could win the race.

Yet, my whole happiness became tied to outside achievements instead of my own internal contentment. It was a cruel attempt to live a happier life. My attention became narrowed and focused upon what the world wanted me to achieve, and the conversations my parents wanted to be having to other people.

Life had become a closely monitored scoreboard where I wanted to be number one. But I would never be able to win. I never admitted the truth I felt deep down that there would be an endless list of desires and personality traits I needed to be. I would never be enough. I would always fall short from everyone's expectations. However, I kept believing that one day, with one more achievement, I could impress the world. I could make my parents proud.

I sat alone on my sofa. Late in the evenings, the blackness of the room reflected the darkness I felt within. Loneliness struck deeply, carving its pain across my entire body. My phone was my one source of light. However, it opened another world, that I was not living. A world full of everyone sharing their best life. I felt the same feelings of inadequacy return.

It was obvious that everyone enjoyed themselves more than me, as I sat by myself in my living room with a packet of paracetamol. I felt like a failure. So I did the only thing I knew how: created a persona of success. An appearance online which gave the perception I was the happiest man on Earth.

Social media became an additional method for me to play my character and curated image through. I solely posted photos of my travels, my extravagant events, racing my car. My money, my achievements, my success. To hide the fact that deep down I was hurt, lost, and lonely. Messages rushed in with people who I had barely spoken to, who desired my lifestyle. A wash of approval. A fix of validation. But then I looked up from my phone, realizing that those highlights were not giving me what I truly wanted deep down. I got the photos I wanted, but I was just satisfying my craving mask, not the real me. As my eyes looked away from the screen, I was met with the dullness of my living room, with the bottle of pills next to me, my salvation.

As much as I was flattered by those who wanted to imitate my moves. Live my life. I was thoroughly confused. I couldn't imagine all those people wanted to be me, when even I didn't want to be myself.

I posted unrealistic images to numb the true feelings of my own life for a fake, artificial reality that was permanently on display. My character would live on. My feelings of failure would remain hidden. I was again chasing the feeling of escapism, wanting to bite down on freedom. Social media was my new pill, my dopamine boosting, obsessive cure.

I experienced an overriding feeling of jealousy deep inside. I had become driven to believe that I was constantly missing out through the array of perfect images that were always available to scroll through on social media. Yet, at the same time, I was convinced that others drinking every weekend were unfocused in attaining their own dreams. Compared to me and my heavily optimized life, tuned for the pursuit of money and success. But then again, I too wanted to get away from my daily existence into a dreamy, intoxicated state.

No matter what life I wanted to live, the internet, social media, and the constant appearances I was being compared against were not going to provide me with the answer. I started to become aware that if my online portrayal wasn't the truth, others would be the same. My own ups and downs were part of our existence that everyone else was also feeling. My own struggles and feelings of unworthiness were in fact a common theme. Social media was not my way out. Just a method of prolonging the pain. Not the long-term solution but a quick temporary fix. The explosive stream of likes and comments would not substitute what I truly wanted deep down. Even if I wasn't sure what that was.

I was always told the grass isn't greener on the other side. But I knew there was a happier and healthier way to live. Away from the temptation and distraction of sharing superficial images on the internet. Away from popping pills in a vague attempt to boost my own internal happiness. Away from other people's opinions on how I should be spending my time. Away from the narrative that I should have been enjoying the fakery that I felt my own life had become.

I was sure there was a better life, that the grass was greener somewhere.

CHAPTER 5:

New Heights

"When you stop chasing the wrong things, you give the right things a chance to catch you."

—LOLLY DASKAL

My exams were done and submitted and the burden on my shoulders lifted. My cupboard full of pills was now mentally in my rear-view mirror, firmly in the distance. I felt alive again. I wouldn't be needing painkillers anymore. And to further boost my self-esteem, I landed the opportunity to meet one of our major clients in New York. I was nineteen and about to sign a huge deal on the other side of the world. *I was killing it.*

Midday struck as my plane touched down into John F. Kennedy Airport. The terminal was covered in a thick layer of snow and ice from the bitterly cold Christmas just gone. As I exited the door of the plane, the sky had cleared. My mind felt the same shift being so far away from my previous existence.

The expansive sky felt so freeing. I could think with all my thoughts, breathe with all the space, and live again. It was like stepping into a whole other world. My own world. My own mind. Which expanded beyond the four walls and long nights it had been confined to.

Staring out the window of the car that took me downtown, seeing the city come into view, I couldn't help but feel a wash of success run over my entire body. Orange light flooded the city providing a powerful backdrop to the dense skyscrapers that glittered ahead. The buildings stood so tall and were so grounded. It reminded me of how strong I had to be to have made it there. To have survived the past months.

I dropped my bags in my suite and breathed. Home for the next month. Taking a look around the room, I reflected on just how surreal this was. The enormous bed, huge bathtub, the skyscrapers outside of my windows. To be in the center of New York City, living the dream I once imagined. The jet-set lifestyle I aspired to. Maybe this was what I pictured years ago in the classrooms staring into the crystal ball. When I stood in front of the mirror, maybe this was what I was aiming for.

I'd been transported into the spotlight of success. My life had hit new heights. And here in New York I was not alone in my views. New York was populated by ambition; it was its only religion. Only here did you apologize for having faith in something other than yourself. Compelled to justify anything other than pure unrelenting focus for your career. I fitted right in.

Strolling down one of the many avenues in the center of the bustling city, as the sun creeped through the narrow gaps in the skyline, you could see the determination etched on everyone's faces. It was imprinted into their very DNA. It was what gave structure to the buildings, what moved the taxis. It was what the city functioned on. The desire for endless desires and progression. The focus on the pursuit for more and better overcame the idea that anything else may exist.

At this point, I hadn't appreciated that there was a point when chasing success transitioned from bravery into foolishness. And that the podium-seeking behavior I desired would become a restless, burning, continual feeling deep inside that would drive me toward pain. I knew that my internal desire to appear triumphant was oppressive, but I always believed any compromise was down to my own lack of abilities or strength. If I did surrender to my fate, I would be seen as a coward. *I would be no failure.*

My eyes glanced to the intense colors on the digital billboard, the neon lights emphasizing the energy and power of the city. I slowly traced the corner of one of the high-rise buildings to the very top, almost losing my bearing as I walked. I wondered in a dazed state, simply stunned, and certainly unable to see the artificial nature of my surroundings. I had been swept up with the glamour and came to realize I had become oblivious to the toxic nature of this ever-chasing ideology.

I'd forgotten any of the deeper meaning that my experiences over the past months might have attempted to teach me. I had become fully engrossed in the glitz and glamor of the bright lights and pulsating excitement of New York. I had been drawn into the pace of the city. It had submerged the struggles I had faced in the previous months. And my mask had become hidden underneath the dazzling magic. No one knew who I was here. I was viewed as a winner through and through in New York. I didn't need to pretend. *At last.*

This was my once-imagined future; I was living my beautiful dream and it tasted so good. How could I disagree with this feeling?

I was free to live how I chose. I had a gold credit card with a twenty-thousand-dollar limit. I got to play and enjoyed the finest of what New York had to offer. Late one evening I strolled into the best Asian restaurant in the city that was lowly lit with a mellow orange aura. A swarm of waiters arrived with a huge display of beautiful ornate dishes that I slowly devoured. I didn't have to be the serious, corporate character I was accustomed to acting out and closely identified with. I was free to do anything I wanted. No one was controlling me here.

I considered that maybe my addiction to pills was simply a temporary resource to accomplish greater goals. To obtain more. Maybe my dependency on them was simply a sign for me to aim even higher. My craving wasn't the pills, but the feeling of success. The happiness this life gave me. The satisfaction I had worked so hard toward. I believed that departing from the world without obtaining a life full of success would be a mistake. That all my sacrifices and hard work would disappear into thin air. My life experience would fade to nothing.

Being here, amongst the energy of the city, the magic that danced in the sky and the carefully sculptured buildings, the importance of success was clearly emphasized in every direction. My mindset re-focused. I was back on track. *More money. More success.*

So I became absorbed in this very ethos. I ignored my wisest instincts and any whispering internal voices that were trying to express their truth. The rhythm of the city was strong and elusive and covered the flicker of any doubts. It was the same pull that I experienced from first stepping inside the towering building back in London. Peaking inside. Peering behind the curtains. My heart had aligned with the vibrating beat of New York, and I enjoyed every second.

Here in New York, I was now free and unattached. No one was able to get to me here. I was away from my previous troubles. In a new place, living a different life. One I liked. The one I had dreamt about. *Why would I want anything different?*

On the intersection of Fiftieth Street and Fifth Avenue, I took the elevator seventy floors up. As the doors drew apart, I was left staring at a priceless view. It was like my office back in London but on steroids. I was even higher. The buildings even more impressive. The views grander and more theatrical. The view stretched for miles, from the Statue of Liberty that I could just make out in the far distance, the Empire State Building that stood tall directly ahead, to the sheer sweeping expansiveness of Central Park. Gazing into the distance, I remembered the time when all I wanted was what I now had in that precise moment.

I felt more protected than ever from the outside world. I was alone looking out onto a city built on the foundation of success. This moment, this feeling was what I was waiting for. I was sure of it. I felt like I'd won the race. I was a winner.

But as my time in New York came to an end, a black, over-sized Chrysler with tinted windows and large leather seats rolled up outside the hotel lobby. I caught my breath, taking one last look around, feeling my feet cemented to the ground. The towering skyscrapers surrounded me. My legs didn't want to move. I was in the city where dreams were made, yet as I absorbed the surroundings one last time, as the city air filled my lungs while the light faded, I couldn't help but feel confused. It felt as if I was leaving behind more than just a city. But an idea. A belief.

I was safe in New York. Detached from the doubters. Miles away from the pills that had controlled my life. Transported far away from the unnecessary office politics and rigid, controlled working hours. The gossip, commutes, and normality of the world were distant. Life here was different. And I was scared. For what was on the other side. Whether things would improve returning home.

I reluctantly climbed into the back passenger seat, and the car door closed firmly shut. As I sunk into the soft leather and looked out the darkened window, I found myself questioning whether this was success. I had made heads turn in the way I longed for by getting to live this lifestyle. Success was projected onto my body from every angle. I was living the lifestyle I dreamed of. Now I had it, I was successful. *But what did this mean?*

I could feel my mask creeping back as it would be required to perform again back in London. The failure I thought I was inside was hidden here, disguised amongst the success I was viewed with in America. As I traveled back across the Atlantic, to an unknown situation, I was left wondering if this was success, after all these years. I contemplated what would happen next. If this was the pinnacle, where would I go from here?

* * *

Touching back down in London, it didn't take me long to start to feel stress and uneasiness. I started to feel the desire for more and better once again.

Later that day, taking the circular motorway into my client's office, hearing the sound of my car's wheels turning continuously against the tarmac, life felt empty. I parked in my usual space, headed past the open foyer, took the stairs to the second floor, and turned right down the corridor. As I gripped the door handle, slowly turning it, my arrival was met with icy darkness.

The meeting room was muted and grey, behind a mist of emptiness. It was like all the energy disappeared, escaping from the crack in the doorway as it opened. I was met with a dimly lit, cramped, windowless box that suppressed every emotion. It was full of the team I was a part of and my client, but it felt empty. All the life had been sucked out the room and it was like being in a vacuum. A consuming sense of dread washed over me at the same time my soul vanished. This initial feeling continued for the duration of the day which felt long and exhausting. I was drained. It was as if the walls in the room were feeding on my energy.

My bosses had unrealistic deadlines that were forced on me. The workload increased. I was supposed to be tending to my client's every wish no matter the time of day. The pressure had mounted, and the expectations raised. I was unhappy.

There was an unnatural darkness in the air as I exited the office and joined the rush hour evening traffic. There was a looming presence. Or maybe it was the absence. Something inside of me that was missing. That the success which was running through my blood had all but vanished. As I sat, unmoving, staring at the brake lights of the car in front, I was left wondering where the beautiful dream I was living just yesterday in New York had gone.

Success was my orientating direction in life. My fuel. Why did I struggle to make that feeling last? I thought I had achieved success, I thought I had bitten down on it, once and for all. What would I have to do next? But instead of blindly continuing onto the next idea and more progress, I thought not about what I was chasing, but why I was so desperate to chase. Why being a chaser felt like my only identity. The outside world was harsh, and I constantly tried to keep up and please everyone. But maybe what I had set out to achieve was in fact an impossible goal.

My mask had become thoroughly confused. It thought it had played its role but now it was back competing in the race again, needing to vanquish my competition and meet my own, even further elevated desires. Although in a slightly disorientated state, the pressure on my character returned, the demands of performance that would be required more extravagant. My mind switched between chasing and not chasing, but the fear of failure deep within always spoke louder.

* * *

I caught the afternoon train to Central London that Saturday ready for the evening performance of a West End show. The sky was cloudy and drizzle was in the air, which was typical for a late January day. The buzz of Christmas and New Year's celebrations were definitely in the past as people rushed into shops to escape the rain, scrolled mindlessly on their phones, focused on their own individualistic actions.

The Tube to Oxford Street was short but gave me the time to just sit and watch the world. Observing the crowds of people rushing through the sliding doors, some catching the very last of the January sales, others eagerly awaiting their theatre show and some heading out for a bite to eat. It felt like I was the only one who appreciated that time was passing. Everyone was too preoccupied to take notice. As I looked around at the brightly colored seat fabric, the beige walls, the red doors, it was as if I was seeing something nobody else could. Something I may not have even experienced myself before. Life. Happening in front of my very eyes.

The lights flickered as we entered the darkness of one of the subterranean tunnels; moisture was just becoming evident on the opened glass windows and there was a rattling sound accompanied by a strong gust of air that swarmed through the carriage. I was aware of the lives of everyone around me and at the same time I was clueless. I was separate and yet I couldn't help but feel that I was contemplating something deeper than I ever had. But this potential new idea was out of reach in front of me too. Too deep, too confusing to grasp. Too ridiculous for me to understand.

It was this moment, as the air rushed past and the track screeched, looking out into the world was different. Everything appeared clearer. The colors more vivid. The sounds stronger. The edges of things sharper and more defined. Facial expressions more detailed. The energy more present. For the first time since I could remember, I was still. Not aimlessly rushing to my finely tuned schedule, attempting to save the extra minute by catching an earlier Tube.

Usually, I was frantic and stressed, always with a list of recurring objectives circling my mind. The slowness of my thoughts appeared to be at odds with the pace at which the rest of the city moved. And the speed to which I had conducted the rest of my life.

But today, I was happily unhurried, taking the time to just look and observe.

I became far too aware of my own obsession with speed. I was always in a panic, rushing, checking my watch, glancing at my crammed schedule, running for the Underground, refreshing my feed. But I couldn't work out where all the extra time I was saving vanished to. I thought the fast pace and intensity of my life was better and helped me achieve what I truly wanted. But my days were busier, longer, harder and my mind over-burdened and exhausted. This unique moment of slowness allowed me to pause, to soak up the environment around me, and to consider my reasoning for rushing around.

I had become swept up with the culture that bought into the idea that if we stay busy enough, the truth of our lives won't catch up with us. So, I spent all my time, energy, and money, creating a flurry, so I never had to meet reality.

However, I had briefly stopped for just long enough to create a quiet emotional clearing which allowed the truth and reality to emerge from its long sleep. I realized I had become so busy trying to please everyone, I forgot to ever ask myself what I wanted.

Momentarily I had escaped my own success-focused bubble. I began to experience a changed outlook. I tried so hard to stay in front of the truth, to not consider how tired and scared and confused and overwhelmed I sometimes felt. But ironically, trying too hard to stay out in front was what wore me down.

I started to question whether the ideas I had grown up around, focusing on money and success, importance and validation, were the right ones. Whether I hurried around, desperately attempting to prevent the truth from catching up to me.

But I didn't have to wait long until I was faced with the truth.

CHAPTER 6:

The One Minute I Realized Everything

"And once the storm is over, you won't remember how you made it through, how you managed to survive. You won't even be sure, whether the storm is really over. But one thing is certain. When you come out of the storm, you won't be the same person who walked in. That's what this storm's all about."

—HARUKI MURAKAMI, KAFKA ON THE SHORE

It was a harmless, unassuming Wednesday morning when I closed the front door and left my house on my journey to work. But I didn't know this day would stay with me for a lifetime. As the radio played on my morning commute, comforted in my car, everything felt so normal. Except today would be the day everything changed.

It didn't take long. Around ten minutes into my journey, tears poured out from nowhere and I suddenly felt out of control. Not from my external world, but from myself. A wash of unusual energy passed over me. Seeping into every crack within me. It was a whole new feeling. An entirely different emotion. But that was the moment I knew something was wrong. By the time my call connected to my mom, tears were streaming down my cheeks.

Unsure on my next moves, and in a dazed state, I drove the short distance to my grandma's house instead of going to work. My vision was clouded with tears filling my eyes and by the time I pulled up outside her house, my face was red, water gushing—I was in trouble. But that was the problem—I wasn't sure what I was crying about. There hadn't been a bad incident, conversation, or moment. I made my way inside, my head dropped lower, facing forward toward the ground and I stumbled, unsure of exactly what was happening.

I just sat down and cried.

It took hours before my tears stopped. Time seemed to slow, stretch, and flatten. I just sat and let it all out. I couldn't identify the cause. And despite the volume of questions I was being asked, I just kept shaking my head. The answer to all the questions was no: something wasn't happening that day that was making me anxious, there hadn't been a bad incident, I wasn't feeling sad. It was the feeling of absolutely nothing. Of being emptied from within. And I was scared whether I was okay.

My head was stuck in a dark place, and I was at a low point and yet my memory recalls being asked whether I would still be heading into work, what I would say about my lateness. But this would have been like jumping off a plane that was crash landing. I couldn't believe that I looked so distressed and exhausted, and still the outside world's desire for me to continue competing would be stronger than ever. That I was at rock bottom and yet there was still so little appreciation for what I was going through.

Everyone believed me to be indestructible, that I could face anything, that nothing would penetrate my skin. The layers of character I had meticulously built up did their job: they covered up my innermost feelings and gave the appearance that I was strong. Except now it wasn't making my life better. It only made it harder to be understood.

I knew differently. I was in trouble, and I was not okay. However, sadly I only sought professional help when my symptoms became too much for me to handle internally. It was only when I was crying my eyes out and thoroughly lost and confused in the world around me, until I finally felt like I could ask for support.

While I sat in the sterile doctor's office that morning, I realized I had never felt lonelier. I was a stranger to myself. While this wasn't new, this was the first time I realized how much I had lost. I had to acknowledge that my carefully crafted character collapsed on me. I paid a high price for not being truthful with myself and the world. Each minute slowly dragged out in front of me as I sat nervously awaiting judgment on my situation.

As I sat opposite my doctor, my face covered with uneasiness, my legs trembled with nerves for what I was about to hear. I wasn't prepared for what came next. I was surprised. My doctor understood what I was going through. It was a relief; she was the first person to see that my outside life was not representative of my inner feelings. She told me how the stresses and pressures had become too much. That I needed to rest and recover. That I had experienced a mental breakdown.

It sounded like something had gone wrong with me. While I sat in the chair in the white walled room, I felt the cold breeze against my arms, and my hairs stood on end. I was still in denial. *How could this have happened to me?*

As I walked out of the doctor's office onto the quiet street, my thoughts and emotions oscillated between pain, anger, and fear. My whole self-image as a successful corporate professional had been reduced to nothing.

Just yesterday I was a young, ambitious, successful, supposedly thriving, up-and-coming professional. I left the doctor a lost, confused, emotional little boy.

I was transported back to that moment I first looked at the building I thought was my home. With the towering heights and glare that shined on the windows. But it turned out the dazzling reflecting panels weren't only preventing me from seeing inside, but stopping the reality from seeping out. Blocking the truth from ever leaving. To give everyone inside the peace that they could still soak in the glamour.

The office foyer I was once stunned by with all its grandeur and magnificence was nothing but an extravagant theatrical show. The ropes that lay in the lobby, the curtains that hung in client meeting rooms, the impressiveness of the building were all an imitation of what they wanted me to see. I was one of the dancing lions in their performance, moving to the rhythm of the puppet masters from above. Too pre-occupied and absorbed by the beautiful room, I never realized where I really was.

A cage.

The trap had been deeply manifested in my mind and I had danced on stage, a character under all my layers of acting and performance. The applause had been deafening. My costume an expensive suit that dazzled under the bright lights alongside the props of my car and bank account.

Until now.

The theater lights had been switched off. The room was empty. I was no longer acting. Now, I sat on the corner of the stage, alone, wondering how I had been so blinded. I was left to face the very thing I ran away from. It was finally time I admitted to myself and to the world...

That I was a failure.

This was the one minute I realized everything. My whole life had become directed by others. I had lost custody over my own mind. The curtains crashed down, the walls smashed behind me, and I was left with the shock of what my life had really been. The choices. The moves. My own wants and desires. They weren't in fact me. They never had been.

The feeling of "me-ness" had completely eroded. My body no longer felt like my own. My mind didn't feel like it was mine anymore. People who have never had a period living with anxiety and panic don't understand that the realness of you is an actual feeling that you can lose. A sense of no return—as if you have suddenly lost something you didn't know you had. That the thing you had to look after was you.

This loss left a scar. I could almost see it. A mark, as if I'd been struck by lightning.

My first encounter with what a mental breakdown meant occurred months earlier where I attended a mental health talk. I can pull from my distant memory an encounter that now feels so vivid, so telling, that I will never forget it. Outside the presentation area, preceding us taking our seats, I overheard a colleague who I didn't know, share her own story. She explained to a small group of colleagues surrounding her that as a result of too much pressure and stress at work, she had been medically signed off after a breakdown.

I was too self-assured to believe this could happen to me. I denied the possibility that I may have been anxious. I hid how I was really was, pretended to be happier and more full of life. Hearing others talk about their experiences made me feel better and worse at the same time. I knew it wasn't just me fighting this battle but maybe I should have realized that there was something that needed addressing. Although I continued my denial about my own mental health deteriorating, I started to realize it was real.

I was scared. Anxiety was my dark ghost that visited without warning. It came no matter the time or day. Always when I least expected it. And ripped me apart. Shadowing my every breath. It filled my chest with shards of glass that hurt with each waking moment. It taunted me until I was forced to accept it as a part of me.

This was a challenge, though, as I felt ashamed and inadequate for being unable to get a grip of my emotions so I buried them deep inside, hoping that by ignoring them they would magically vanish. I was so used to handling pressure and naïve in thinking my feelings and emotions wouldn't become too much and take control of me. But there was a real cost in leaving these thoughts unexpressed. They accumulated deep inside. It was hard to admit I was in this place, given the surface-level of perfection I had. That while everything looked like it had gone well, internally I was wounded.

Despite hiding my true feelings, never fully sharing how I was actually was with all the rigor and detail I should have, there were still conversations where I tried too hard to take off my exterior facade, to let my heart speak its truth. Whether it was family, managers at work, and a handful of others, I hinted at the fact that I was struggling. The words may have been different. But the underlying message was the same.

But I was always talking, laughing, and joking so no one really realized what was going on underneath the surface. So these conversations only exaggerated my feelings that I should just continue. People only notice when it's too late. Change only happens when things become too much. They didn't realize that the reason I talked and joked was because I was afraid.

It began to dawn on me that my overcompensation and fake bravado were really just another manifestation of the failure I thought I felt inside. I had relentlessly kept it hidden from the world. But now the failure had revealed itself.

* * *

Coming home that day felt strange. Everything smelled the same. Looked the same. Felt the same. But I was different. The contrast between who I left the house as that day and when I returned home was like comparing night and day, and it all happened in the space of hours.

My breakdown was a deep, hard-hitting painful actualization at the end of a slow and agonizing path of wrong turns and poor decisions that led my mind, and who I was, astray. It was rock bottom. However, the days that followed were equally as painful and were missing the adrenaline that got me though the initial morning. Everything from my life had suddenly vanished. My outside existence was now as empty as my feelings inside.

Everything I had known, believed and trusted had fallen away—leaving an empty, vacant space. I existed in this limbo emptiness for weeks.

As I sat alone on my sofa, I was left to face my darkest of demons. A lot of the burden was self-imposed, and I had become a prisoner of my own ambition. I always worked harder, pushed for more, but proving my worth became the thing that brought me down. I was left to piece myself back together and finally reconnect with my truth. I was not aware of how much was trapped and locked up inside of me from the slow-burning pain of not living a life true to myself.

At just twenty years old, my dream was tied to what others desperately wanted me to strive for. And it wasn't supposed to be like this. But I and I alone was left to pick up the pieces. It was going to be down to me to make the changes.

My heart and mind fractured into a thousand tiny pieces, and I needed to believe that there was a truer, more expansive and fulfilling version of myself out there. I needed to believe that when your life becomes a cage, you can loosen the bars and reclaim your freedom.

However, I was left with the terrifying thought that if being rich and successful doesn't stop my insecurities and make me feel happy—maybe the issue was me. The solution to my problem seemed beyond reach: a boat, lost in the fog, drifting further and further away.

As much as I was filled with sadness, my tears slowly rolling down my cheeks, alone and confused, I would soon learn that this moment was the best thing that happened to me. It was the moment I woke up and could suddenly see for myself again. Pain so deep that I would be forced to make changes. An abrupt awareness so powerful it couldn't be denied any longer. The same place I felt maximum distress, provided me with my most important moment. The stone fell hard enough to make the ripple last a lifetime.

I returned to work and started to have conversations about my experiences. But I was thought to have been fixed. That I was no longer experiencing any mental battles. Those two weeks alone on my sofa at home as well as going in and out of therapy sessions was the cure. The miracle solution. As if nothing had ever happened. I knew I couldn't keep going, dealing with the toxic misery my life had become, the daily struggles. I couldn't keep going, not like this.

I attempted to share my story. To be vulnerable. To be honest about everything I was feeling for once. Instead of being hidden behind the facade of my character of my endless desires, progress, and achievements. But sharing my story, my experience, always felt like such a battle. It was trying to go against the very fabric of my bones.

It was hard for others to see my truth deep inside. I was still perceived to be the unstoppable, courageous, fearless characterized version of myself. I also struggled to admit to others that my whole persona, everything they had ever seen, was a lie. I had to be open and honest. *I just knew I couldn't pretend anymore.*

My life-long training, the layers of performance, had always taught me to put my best foot forward, to pretend my problems don't fully exist, and delude my own mind into a false sense of security. So I was not used to confronting the internal conflicts my mind was consumed with. But I had to try. I thought opening up would make me weak, but I realized it actually made me strong. I finally decided to take off my mask. To reveal my full self to the world. I was my own person. I could do things my way.

* * *

Back when I freely roamed the streets, sat in my classes, and played football in the park, I looked through my innocent eyes, and started to build up views on the world and slowly formed ideas. I saw a society desperate for success and riches. I wanted the same. But deep down I knew I could be better and greater and attain even more happiness. I interpreted this conclusion to mean that I needed to find a better job and obtain a fancier car and more money. I thought doing more of what others were doing was the thing to make everything right in my own life.

Having sat in the darkness of my own mind, having questioned everything I thought I knew, there was some truth from when I squinted all those years ago, with the belief that I could attain more happiness. The difference is that now I realize I needed to think differently and head in the opposite direction to others. Not to fill it with more of the misery and drudgery that was already present, but to find happiness and enjoyment through doing something everyone else wasn't.

CHAPTER 7:

A Period of Enlightenment

"Nature does not hurry, yet everything is accomplished."

—LAO TZU

The airport was a world of its own. Full of unique human stories and backgrounds, that all intersected at a single point of space and time. I always looked forward to the physical barrier flying created with the rest of the world; the thirty thousand feet of air between me and the earth. A vacuum from the pain I had been feeling on the ground. An isolated moment away from the distractions, bosses, unnecessary comments, notifications, work calls, and disagreements. Nobody could get hold of me and hurt me up there.

I needed this trip. To experience something other than the turbulence that had filled my life over the past months. To live differently, to allow my mind to be opened to the world of possibilities. To get outside of the corporate bubble that intoxicated my life. To leave everything I thought I knew behind and realize the endless prospects the world offered. It was a chance to adapt to the changing surroundings, tackle new challenges, and discover traits about myself that could only be truly invoked by the dynamics of travel.

As the plane turned toward the runway and aligned itself with the straight row of bright, delicately placed lights down the center of black tarmac, the engines bellowed, and the wing flaps lowered. A soothing force pushed me back into my seat, comforting me while I watched the speed of the outside world going past. I took a deep breath. My head was softly pushed into the pillow while music filled my ears, which drowned out the sounds of the jet engines. I rested my head back and tilted it toward the window as I watched the world I knew disappear. Escaping the life that had caused me so much stress and anxiety that I was leaving behind, for the world in the air.

I was surprised how built-up Bali airport was. It definitely wasn't the tropical, rice field island I had expected. My family and I met our driver, who had come from our accommodation a couple of hours away, and swiftly jumped into the back of the van to escape the beaming heat for the cooler air-conditioning. As we headed further away from the Southern Coast where the airport and all-inclusive hot spots were situated, the true magic of Bali began to emerge. It became clear how spiritually orientated this magical island was and the significance that this played in their lives. Colorful scented flowers lay on the pavements and various entrances, aromatic scents filled the air, with patches of smoke arising, dancing in the faint breeze.

* * *

From the moment I stepped out of the car in Ubud and saw the luscious surroundings and felt a rush of relaxation over me, I could tell this was the life and break I was looking forward to. The days would be so different: there would be doors to open, streets to cross, fresh coconuts to sip, secret pathways to discover, people to brush past, rice fields to roam in, exotic scents to inhale, local crafts to admire, waterfalls to explore. But at that moment, the unknown was all I needed. The undetermined possibilities of what was to come, but knowing I was free.

I strolled through the streets and along the sides of expansive greenery with growing crops. I was both physically and mentally miles away from what I knew. Detached from my previous existence. An escape to somewhere better.

The surroundings were full of intricate, ornate structures with red tiled terracotta roofs, each with its own unique shape. High rice canes rose from the ground in all directions. Palm trees sporadically around. In fact, greenery filled the views, contrasted against the orange-and-peach-colored buildings that were scattered in the distance. Along the small corridor-like roads which created a sort of maze, motorbikes weaved, slowing briefly around a tight corner.

From a spontaneous encounter in the street late one evening, we exchanged details with a local who ran private tour trips. The following day we headed with him to a temple tucked in the countryside and observed the rituals being carried out and absorbed the restful nature of the place.

We talked about my very recent experiences with stress and the difficulty I was having in relaxing. Our guide spoke about feeling similar emotions and that in order to resolve the tension, he finds a spot in the jungle river and lets the water float past, closes his eyes, and relaxes in nature's hand. It sounded magical. It was the kind of therapy and tranquility that I longed for. Watching my struggles disappear, floating away into the distance, being comforted by nature around me.

It was a beautiful moment. His ways of dealing with the issues he faced were poetic compared to mine. Struggles are universal, of course, but our methods in dealing with them couldn't be more different. I had grown up around a culture that desperately attempts to overlook and internalize issues instead of Bali's openness and realism with the issues every human faces. I had been so used to the ideas of popping pills, carrying on and manning up compared with this beautiful alternative of a blissful moment amongst nature. I envied the freedom he lived with to be able to connect with his environment and find peace.

Later that day, when patches of clouds were just starting to group together in the otherwise clear sky, we traveled to a waterfall nestled behind a small rice village in the surrounding area. With swimming trunks on, we headed down some steps cut out in the rocks, and onto the waterfall itself. Freezing cold water thundered down, crashing onto us and the smoothed dark rocks around us. In the middle of a patch of jungle, we were the only ones there, experiencing the magical beauty. Carefully balancing my body and dodging the large volumes of water that were plummeting below, I started to climb up the waterfall.

The sound of the rushing water deafened me, and it wasn't long until all other sounds faded from my senses. Looking down at the pool of water below, with the bend of the river curling around the jungle floor, I got a sense of what our tour guide experienced. Feeling beautifully small, my feelings drifting eloquently around the curving bends of the river and away from my mind. Feeling stillness and serenity instead of frustration and hopelessness.

My actions were always full of determination and discipline as I had become well-accustomed to wrestling and bending the universe to my will through sheer force. I had to be perfect at all times. But that moment, meditatively sitting amongst the waterfall, was perfect just the way it was. I wanted to accept myself. My striving for perfection was getting in the way of the beauty of life and this quest destroyed me in the process.

As the sun faded with each day, and our trip progressed, we took a tightly packed van across the island. We threw open the sliding door and clambered inside where seats were piled on top of each other and there was a strong scent of sweat that filled the air. The van was, in ways, iconic with its brightly colored painted exterior, a small ladder running down one side of the back and the van's body stylishly lowered so it just hovered over the wheels. Our luggage was loosely strapped to the roof. The roads would be of all shapes, sizes, and terrains and the number of hours we would be squished, my legs forced to press up against the seat in front of me, was unknown. It was going to be a long journey.

The scenery was stunning. From the tops of the palm trees, steep, sudden inclines that rose above the island, to the multitude of local villages with locals in the rice fields with their straw collie hats and plows. Dedicated to working the land, with the lines of green blooming rice plants that lined the fields on either side of the narrow roads. So much life was happening on the other side of the glass. But this time, I wasn't letting the glare prevent me from being a part of it. I wasn't feeling high or mighty, acting above the normality. I was a part of it.

Young children played in the street with an array of objects, fresh markets sprung from the street corners, selling fresh local produce. Elders could be seen on their porches, sitting, watching the world. There wasn't a phone in sight. Not an unachievable ambition held. Success, at least in the way I knew it, was not their orientating direction.

As the greenery flashed past, and the magic of the island continued to reveal itself, I realized the journey in life was everything. There was no mountaintop. No pinnacle. I was always so sure there would be something better around the corner. Over the next hill. But this way of thinking had kept me trapped in a never-ending quest for a life I wasn't living.

Seeing life play out in front of me here allowed me to recognize the game, the trick, the insanity, the carrot dangling on the end of the stick, the insatiable human hunger, the unquenchable thirst and chronic dissatisfaction, the attempt to fill a spiritual hole with external things.

The race was a lie.

Unparalleled winning and achieving everything I had ever dreamt did not secure me with perfect happiness and ultimate bliss. Life was not a finely tuned game to win. It was a process of learning, growth, and most importantly, acceptance.

I couldn't believe it had taken me until now to appreciate that I had been trapped by the ambitions placed on me. Imprisoned by my own ideas that there was a reason to keep climbing in anticipation for something better. But staring into the world for what it was should have been enough.

* * *

After the long journey, we took the hour-long flight to a neighboring island of Bali called Flores where we began the next part of our trip. The morning after our arrival, the sun crept over the mountainous backdrop, spreading orange light over the coastal town. This was accompanied by the sounds of religious morning prayer that filled the air from the surrounding mosques and temples which were faintly visible from the balcony of our small wooden apartment, located on the hill overlooking the bay. Ships moved around with grace, the water rippling and leaving a disappearing mark of their path. The air had a beautiful freshness, with a dash of salt from the sea, that ran calmly through my hair. As the sun continued to reveal itself, the sounds reflected around the curvature of the bay.

My senses heightened, absorbing this whole different way of life. It opened my mind to the thousands of different eye-opening possibilities. And that I too could live differently.

But there was also a sense of peace that had been missing almost my entire life. A sense of serenity in my mind. My head was clear to think its own thoughts. My eyes could see the world for what was in front of me.

Later that morning, when the town started to wake, we boarded a small boat full of backpackers for a four-day trip around various Indonesian islands. We would venture around multiple isolated and tropical patches of paradise. What followed, as we departed from Flores, was a spectacular array of grassy headlands, stunning wildlife, white sand beaches and luscious, crystal blue waters. We snorkeled with rays and turtles, climbed waterfalls, explored islands from picturesque postcards, trekked looking for Komodo dragons, drank local coffee, and sat back and relaxed on the deck, watching the vistas of Indonesia.

The change in my environment transported me into a whole new world of possibilities. Opened new entire parts of my mind. Expanded my horizons. Suddenly I sensed excitement, adventure, and challenge in my body. *Would it be possible to fill more of my life with this?*

Under the cover of darkness one morning, way before the sun was ready to make its arrival, we took tender boats to the shore of Padar: a small island located between Komodo and Rinca Islands. No one lived there but this morning we were going to be watching the sun break from its sleep.

Padar had a beautiful, dragon-like spine that was curved with a mix of white sand beaches and rocky terrain. The crisp blackness of the sky elevated the sparkle in the stars which were shining brightly but were soon to be invisible with the morning light. We climbed up to one end, viewing the rest of the landscape from the high point, overlooking what would soon become a beautiful vista when the sun entered the scene.

An ambient orange glow slowly filled the expansive sky, with the sun itching to burst through the horizon, beaming warm rays over the remote and beautiful paradise we were standing on. We were on the edge of a new day, on the edge of life. The vastness of space and time suddenly was apparent, and I felt so tiny in comparison to the rest of the world. The cosmic scope and scale of the planet with its intricate complexity was so much bigger than who I was and what I had been dealing with.

I suddenly felt so insignificant as the almighty powerful sun showed its face. The color with all its richness booming over the landscape. I could just stand and watch the unfolding of the events in the world. Not needing to imprint a view of what I wanted or how things should be. Not wishing to control anything outside of me. Realizing everything was so much bigger than me, my problems, and sorrows. The universe didn't expect me to be this certain type of person. Understanding that my demons were a faint humming inside my head. That the real world doesn't have this internal monologue creating undesired noise telling it what to do and how to feel. I could escape this too if I wished.

I needed to remove the cover of darkness from my own life, so I could begin to see the power of the light. Zone out from the voices that were controlling my inner mind. Understand that I had the strength to change. It was possible to shift my direction.

As I stood by myself, staring ahead into the horizon over the still water, I acknowledged I was not, in fact, alone. Here on this isolated space away from civilization, I had reconnected with who I was again. Finally became focused on what was important to me. I watched the waves crash against the rugged rocks below. Looking around, everything here was so natural and honest. Maybe I could be who I actually was again too.

As a child I had crafted a particular identity. I decided there was a specific way I had to be in order to both survive and thrive in my environment. But standing in complete stillness, I could see this behavior conflicted with the truth of what I was actually thinking and feeling.

My whole life had always belonged to someone else. First, the expectations on me. Then, ambitions born of competing with everyone around me. And always, always the fact that I tried to be someone who I truly wasn't. But here, I felt for the first time in my life that I belonged.

I didn't have to do anything different. I didn't have to be anything different. In that moment, I just was.

I was enough.

I really felt as if I was on the edge of the world. I longed to stay on this deserted island. I didn't want to leave. I'd had a period of enlightenment. Away from the world I was told to love. Away from the stresses, frustrations, comparison-obsessed, hyper-connected, intensity. Away into a world of my own. This moment, looking out into the beautifully sculpted landscape ahead, was too great a lesson for me to keep ignoring. This realization somehow seemed stronger than the years of culture and conditioning that had suppressed my way of thinking.

CHAPTER 8:

Trusting My Deepest Instincts

"I am no longer accepting the things I cannot change. I am changing the things I cannot accept."

—ANGELA DAVIS

Padar Island impacted me. As I stood and watched the world unfold that morning, my awareness had been shifted. Everything looked different now. And this moment forced me to make changes in my life.

I sat staring at the clock. One second. Two seconds. Three seconds. My eyes flickered with the boredom as yet more dull spreadsheets stared back at me. I'd returned home to work and I felt my whole body ache, not from the pain of sitting at a computer all day, but from the pull on me to live a different life.

Physically I sat at my desk but mentally I was miles away. But an email notification or work difficulty always threw me right back into reality. I wanted to get away from my daily monotonous existence. The white walls, the airless rooms, the sinking feeling that continued to consume me, were reminders that the life I was living was not true to who I was deep within.

This feeling fueled my desire to move and transition onto a new path. As much as I doubted my ideas and opinions, I knew that deep inside there was something I wanted to chase. A big leap I wanted to make. An idea I wanted to work on. I wasn't prepared to keep waiting for change.

But as much as those moments brought great clarity, I still struggled to identify where I should leap to. The offices I sat in drained the very sentiment of being human from me. My ideal vision became muffled and blurred. I had no clue of my guiding direction anymore. I was simultaneously being pulled in a million directions, but I always came back empty when I thought about what I wanted. The crystal ball from years before was desolate. My own mind told me nothing. It was like all those moments years ago, feeling like I needed to make a decision, a choice, but this time the solution was waiting on me. I was deciding.

My mind wandered across the tabs on my screen, out of the window, at the blank derelict walls, at the mundane carpet, and at me, with my crisp collared shirt, my shining leather shoes. *Is this who I want to be? Make a change.*

Things were different; after all my experiences I had seen there was a better life than the one I was living. But I was comfortable in my current position. I still received crazy acknowledgment for my supposed heroic achievements despite openly informing people I not only struggled but was permanently dissatisfied and almost constantly filled with unhappiness. I would have to mentally prepare for the barrage of pessimism, stupidity, and craziness that I would be labelled with.

There was a beautifully laid out path ahead, perfectly trodden. An accepted route. And here I was, wanting to stray into the brambles, the unknown. Underneath the layers of personality and persona that had controlled my life and kept me tied to the straight, narrow conditioning in the world, I had discovered an innateness to explore. I knew that I needed to overcome the resistance that would stand in my way. The feeling that this was the avenue I wanted to venture down was strong. Deep down I trusted it would be worth it.

I knew my previous experiences were truths that were propelling me to change. I knew that building a fortune and creating outward success was going to leave me departing this life unfulfilled. *Take the risk. Make the jump.*

And I had to learn to accept that I no longer knew what lay ahead. I would have to travel through the black void of nothingness. A derelict desert. A blank canvas. Not only facing the dark expansive void but realizing that I no longer knew who I was. I wondered if I had ever known.

I would have to face the emptiness of unfilled time. I didn't know where I was going to be and what I was going to be doing. Life up until this point had been a process of careful planning with great detail, thought, and precision. Each decision designed to move me one step further in the game, one rung up the ladder. One place higher in the race. Relentlessly moving forward and upward.

I couldn't continue to trap myself. Not now. After everything. So I trusted my deepest instincts.

I quit.

As I departed from the towering building that day, I felt a crushing weight combined with liberating freedom. I departed from my once-imagined beautiful dream turned nightmare. I had spent years chasing the wrong path. I hid my true self underneath layers of performance. I had been so wrong for so long. There had been a huge mental cost that I felt burdened with walking out the revolving doors. But I was also relieved. The weight evaporated off my shoulders.

I left my ego inside the building that devoured it and walked down the marble stairs, one step at a time. My feet felt cemented on the ground; there was no more distance between me and the outside world. As I looked around for one last time, I felt all my emotions and senses flood back. I had finally aligned my inner world with my external life. There was going to be no more hesitation, waiting, or delaying in reclaiming control over my life.

Looking back at the building, I couldn't appreciate the full extent of the journey I had been on. This was the place it had all began. And the moment where the pain and lies would end. I had transformed back into an outside observer—not yet able to make sense of what I had left behind.

* * *

I allowed my new outlook to sink in. And prepared to tell the world about what I had learned, my journey of discovery, and my decision. Yet, my whole environment in London suffocated me once again. No one would listen, understand, or take note. Nothing had shifted in the world around me.

It didn't matter who I spoke to—mentors, friends, colleagues—the answer was always the same. That I was the crazy one. Nothing I could say could change their entrenched views. That I could do anything different. I could feel my whole perspective being slowly constrained by the ever-present constant doubt and narrowing. Those closest to me desperately trying to help but only ended up pushing me further away.

I was the outcast and nothing I could say would change their mind.

I sensed that my views would never be known. That I would forever be alone in my way of thinking. My own formations of the world were young but nevertheless had the strength to pervade through the stormy seas that lay in my wake. The challenge was weathering the storm amongst the pure stupidity that I became incessantly labeled with. The sheer naivety it appeared I acted with.

The conversations that I suppose were expected to get me in line and wake up to the way life worked, instead only exaggerated my feelings for the complete opposite. Breaking away from the close-minded, unnecessary difficulties I had been so blindly accustomed to.

My entire ideas and direction about life had reversed but instead of receiving praise and acknowledgment for my internally profound realizations, a barrel of unfair narratives came headfirst at me. Destroying the very notion that I had located some unknown truth and radical wisdom and replaced it with the opinion that it was, in fact, pure foolishness. That it was impossible to have uncovered a better way to live. That an unconventional idea could be correct.

But why would they agree? Years of their life were spent chasing a life that was firmly fixated on the future. How could they give up now? It wasn't that I was upsetting some long-held view: it was their entire life, a requirement for their own hope. Here I challenged a world that was never once questioned. Believed in a better way where it was made clear there could only be one way. So I became a glitch in the game that needed to be eliminated. Or a target to be persuaded otherwise. I had found a cheat code to the race, and I had to be stopped.

To the outside world, my decision appeared reckless and stupid, so I became vilified for it by those around me who pushed for me to compete and climb. The words I spoke were contradicting the minds of everyone I knew. But I absorbed the role of villain-rebel, accepted it, and grew into it. It too became a part of my new identity. But I enjoyed the liberty it gave me, so I played it.

Being unorthodox had defied the logic of the whole value system. Going against the entire culture. There was a dull, insistent tug on me based on the bombardment of conversations and messages, telling me I shouldn't do what my heart was saying. Messages from co-workers, managers, friends, family, and even strangers, that I had been immersed in since the day I was born. That were training me to distrust my own wisest instincts.

My environment was still heavily designed around fighting for more prestige and status. I strolled down a quiet, private residential street, tucked around the corner from the expensive Kensington shops, with the palatial cream-stoned town houses and the neatly trimmed trees that lined the pristine pavement. But it was clear when looking around that doubt and nervousness about my newly found beliefs crept into my mind like an unwelcome guest.

Wandering the millionaire streets in the land of the elite and famous made that desire for success deep within grow stronger. The world wanted to put me back in the same cage I escaped from.

The power of the money on display pulled my emotions in a million directions. My innermost ideas were suddenly distracted. A strong desire within became attracted to all the glitter and glamor involved in continuing on the money-driven, success-pursuing path. The fancy houses, Monaco weekends, helicopter trips. As much as my experiences had taught me this was a trap designed to keep me imprisoned, this lifestyle still danced in front of my eyes.

I attempted to block out the messages and alluring distractions around me. The super cars spitting petrol. The fancy houses with large chandeliers. Distracting my inner North Star.

My inner voice whispered back to me. *Trust your instincts.* The battle raged on inside though, throwing heavy punches. All my logic screamed that I had made a mistake. I had been told my whole life to strive, work, earn, conquer, and climb. But that feeling, my truth, humming deep inside was so strong.

I had changed forever. I had overcome the resistance. I wasn't going to listen to the rest of the world anymore.

I opened my eyes and saw I was not alone. So many people, as we grow up, are asked to be who we are not. We convince ourselves that we are pursuing worthwhile goals, but in the process, we become experts at hiding from ourselves. But I had awoken to how I had been artificially filling my life with material possessions and short buzzes of adrenaline and dopamine.

The journey of change was painful as I had wandered too far, changed too much to bear any resemblance to the wealth-focused, success-orientated young man everyone remembered. So I contended with the fact that people could no longer identify who was talking. I had ripped off my sewn-on labels. I hadn't realized the strength of my own character until now, and the courage I would need to withhold to disentangle myself from my identity, which had been intentionally programmed from afar, long ago. Cut into my skin. Combatting it was the only option. But it wouldn't be easy.

These beliefs that had formed became my own limiting factor. My archenemy. A hard-coded, brainwashed set of ideas that dug their way deep into my subconscious mind which ended up driving who I was. I wanted to drift from the status and performance-orientated beliefs I was known for. Escape the mental cage of believing my own identity was in fact permanent and fixed.

After all, everything I had worked for, all my painful memories, had been to allow myself this one privilege: to see and experience more truths than those handed to me and to use those truths to construct my own mind, make my own choices, and form my own opinions and values. If I gave in and allowed myself to be swayed by anything different, I wouldn't have just lost an argument but control and agency over my own mind. This was the price I was being asked to pay. What those around me wanted to take away was not anything wrong with me; it was the very thing that made me who I was.

CHAPTER 9:

The Scary Leap

"Our greatest ability as humans is not to change the world, but to change ourselves."

—GANDHI

Today, my life would change. The transformation was inevitable. How could I not do anything differently? And although I wasn't sure where the shift would take me, I knew it would transport me somewhere better. Maybe not somewhere new but it would allow me to rediscover the truest, purest version of myself. My core essence. My internal being.

When my mind wandered free in the classrooms all those years ago, when I daydreamed about all the opportunities, all the things I could do with my life, when I gazed out the window at my desk but longed for something different, I dreamed of freedom.

I thought freedom was an amount of money, number of followers, lifestyle, an Instagram highlights reel. I thought it was the ability to feel good all the time. To be happy. To be rich. For the world to consider me as successful. I was tricked into believing that I needed to meet milestones, reach heights, and to climb in order to feel like I could make my own choices, to pursue my own ideas, to be who I really wanted: to be free. But now I realize I'd been liberated all this time. Freedom was a state of mind. I was free all along.

I had tried to build a life that embodied the very soul of chasing, conquering, and climbing. I had worked so hard on my exams, on improving, on gaining experience that would allow me to progress. But I had persisted on seeing the truth. So I stepped away from the life I once imagined and started to rethink about the life I wanted to live. I had taken the long and arduous journey upstream of the meandering river of life, to work out why I kept falling in. I had shattered into a thousand pieces and as I slowly picked myself up and put myself together, I realized I was still whole. But a new shape and size. In fact, I had become who I was once again. That childhood voice that was previously me, became my own again.

* * *

As I slowly closed the door, hearing the definitive click as it shut, I slowly turned the key. I was locking the door of my previous life but opening a whole new world. The journey to the airport seemed to last a lifetime. A tear drop delicately slid down my cheek as I stared out the window. I saw my whole life flash by in front of me. The building standing so tall, the tiny white pills, my beating heart in New York, the pain of my breakdown, the magic of Indonesia. To the days I could run for miles as a child before any of this started.

As the car pulled off the motorway, and the airport terminal came into view, a plane lowered, ready to land. I wanted to reclaim that childhood voice, the dreamy imagination where nothing seemed impossible, where everything was a hazy possibility, an opportunity, a beautiful moment.

I repeated to myself: change, change, change. More as a soothing chant than a warning sign. This reminded me that I had to do this. And this time, I didn't hear the nagging self-doubt that followed every personal resolution. Because I whole-heartedly believed in my decision. I knew I wouldn't fail this time. I couldn't because it's change now or change never. The idea that I would remain the old version of myself, forever, is what I found truly depressing.

The momentum of my past, the life I knew, the security, the safety, the known, the comfortable, was a force that had prevented me from making this move. My best intentions had become thwarted by external forces I had set into motion a long time ago. The bad decisions led to a momentum that was difficult to stop. Until now.

As I moved through the terminal, edging closer to the plane that would transport me away, it felt like I was leaving more than just a place behind. Instead, I had retreated from a collection of experiences that shaped me. That molded me. But in reality, I was getting back to who I was before the world told me who to be. I was unlearning the years of conditioning, rethinking about what my true goals were, and reimagining the life I could live.

The cold air of London raised the hairs on my arms. I shivered. The tunnel connecting the terminal and the plane stretched for an eternity, narrowing toward the port key that would fly me to where I needed to be. Walking down the passage jutting out from the sharp glass edges of the terminal, I levitated between two worlds.

My mind raced with thousands of thoughts, but one was on the top of my mind. Fear had always been such a controlling element of my life. Although it must have appeared that on the surface, I had huge tolerance for risk and uncertainty, for being able to make this leap. It was more of a case that I was so certain that I couldn't let any more time go on with letting the unknown dictate my decisions and choices. I had always been a young man who was gripped by distress: fear of not being the best, of not being important, of not being rich, of not looking good, of not fitting in. And most prominently, the fear of failure.

I walked, continuing past a curve in the tunnel, moving in a space that connected the passage between my old life back at the terminal gate and my soon-to-be new one. The plane door was just steps in front of me. My body headed through the door and my mind soon followed. I realized instantly that fear was not real. It had hijacked my dreams until this moment.

Change is hard, painful, and as far as your brain is concerned, change is not safe. Many people wondered if I was crazy in leaving my cushy corporate gig for an uncertain venture. Maybe I only had eyes for the opportunities, and that's what downplayed the risks. But I also understood I can do hard things. This time I didn't resort to numbing my emotions with drugs. It isn't hard because I'm weak or flawed. It is hard because human life is just difficult, and I am a human finally doing life right.

The forward motion of the plane pushed through the resistance ahead and left in its wake a faint but visible mark of the path I had traveled. The plane's nose, along with me, carving the direction of the future. I was leaving behind a tiny speck that became even smaller as we gained momentum in the sky. But the further I progressed, the greater the impact I realized my experiences had on me. Maybe greater than I had ever known. But I also noticed I wasn't really leaving anything behind.

I had everything I needed. I had myself.

I looked out of the small window and watched the wispy clouds dance in the open space, the sheer expansiveness of the sky similar to how I was feeling inside. Feeling so beautifully free. There was so much separation and detachment from the world, but also from my past life.

I could see some cuts on the windows as a result from the thousands of miles of flying. I too had some mental marks. But I now see through the window clearly. Without letting those scars alter my thinking, my beliefs, my future. In fact, those scratches are the very thing that made me realize I needed to be here today—that allowed me to appreciate I needed to reclaim my true self.

I knew this was right. I no longer needed to question myself or fight my inner voice. I finally let it speak. And I listened. My internal voice became my guiding direction.

I had to take the scary leap. I was changing so much, and this bold move would also transport me thousands of miles away from London. I knew deep within a place didn't define who I was. I wasn't under the illusion that a different location could change my feelings. But I was trying to get closer to the true me. And to do this, I needed to live in a culture that celebrated the same values I had cultivated. A place that prioritized health over wealth. Community over conformity. Freedom over money.

The plane was my vehicle for change. A transportation method. The huge, heavy metal object flying smoothly and seamlessly in the open sky. An innovative masterpiece. A symbol of connection. It would be my way of getting to the place I felt like I most belonged. A location that I felt an inner pull to. Not a pedestal or podium. Not the glossy heights of shining towers. Not a place to obtain money and material possessions. Not a place to numb my true feelings. But somewhere I could be at peace. A place of happiness. A place that would welcome me with open arms. A place that I could be amongst the very everyday movements of life.

A place I could call home.

My body felt a sense of relief as I slowly emerged from the plane, taking each step one at a time until I was on solid ground. The humidity and heat were powerful, but I was stunned at the serenity that ran over every atom in my body, and the calmness of my mind. *I had made it.*

I let my imagination explore all the possibilities in front of me. Dreaming of everything I could do now. In my new life. That inner childhood voice that longed for travel, for freedom, had been rediscovered and my actions were making the most of this lost-then-found voice.

* * *

Hanoi was a capital with a purpose. Within a country that had an energizing, renewed sense of excitement that packed its streets, crept through the cracks in the walls and intensely filled the air. Motorbikes lined the sidewalks and swarmed the streets in masses. Walls that lined the streets were painted full of vivid color. Cables precariously hung out of the buildings in a chaotic logic. Small plastic tables and chairs lounged outside local street food stalls. Narrow alleyways created a maze of hidden passages. Local markets with an exotic collection of unknown foods nestled within the veins of the city.

My senses were hit with an array of newness. Excitement with all the sights and smells that washed over me, I was able to piece together a completely different perception of reality.

I had entered a city so much brighter and busier than the cold and dark skyline of London that had been my previous existence. The optimism and vitality of Hanoi overwhelmed me, with its possibilities, the spirit, the surging adrenalin of four-and-a-half-million dreams being pursued simultaneously with little concern for what is stirred up in their wake. I couldn't have been further from my old life.

London always had the sense that my dreams were narrowed to the expectations that were pressed on me. A certain dullness where your imagination was suppressed by the drudgery of what life was supposed to look like. There was a smog that filled the air, but it was more an idea that intended to reduce my aspirations and imagination. But I escaped!

Swapping my usual setting and outlook, my head turned down, staring intensely at the electronic screens while mindlessly scrolling, rushing with my eyes firmly on my watch, from always being in a future moment, I had been so accustomed to sleepwalking, but Vietnam shook me out of my dazed state. Here, simply walking down the street, I couldn't take my eyes off the craziness, the beauty, the life. Gratitude dripped from every corner, love oozed from everyone in such an accommodating manner, and the momentary presence of locals was clear in their every action.

With every glance, I became infected by the abundance of vibrancy and the smiles that were always on display. The happiness that filled everyone's lungs spread to me. There was an upbeat rhythm that was the primary force which created a sense of magic—the beauty of life. The fact we were alive. Not just alive, but fully living.

CHAPTER 10:

My New Life

"No matter how hard the past, you can always begin again."

—BUDDHA

Sun streams through the open windows filling the coffee shop on the corner of Nha Chung Street with light. Dawn stretches its radiant body across the sky. My back slowly warms with the morning rays. Roosters screech, contesting with each other in the distance. I can faintly hear the humming activity of beeps of unseen scooters to the ticks of an old clock. A new day was unfolding.

This is my new life. I feel content. Sat alone with my fresh local coffee waking me from my sleep, observing the world slowly, motion into action as the sun reaches higher into the sky. I feel energized and ready to live the day. I've found projects and work that genuinely excite me. Arriving at this point has been a real journey, but now I have a real impact every day on topics and issues I care about. Whether that be campaigning for stronger messaging around mental health. Advising the next generation of leading companies on their strategy. Or having calls with young entrepreneurs, like me, wanting to make a difference in the world.

I focus on building my business in a sustainable, balanced way. I'm determined to only work on projects that align to my core beliefs, and that are making the world a better place, in ways where I can add real value. I put myself first. My health is never compromised. My mind has clarity. And ironically, I am making more money than ever before despite this not being a reason for my motivations and actions.

All along, right from the start, my journey was really about finding meaning in my life. I thought climbing the corporate ladder and receiving approval would fulfill me with an ever-lasting immense satisfaction. But meaning isn't found somewhere in the external world. It's deep within. Through heart-felt connections with like-minded individuals, having autonomy over my own schedule, and being able to choose challenges that are intrinsically motivating to me.

As morning turns to midday, I stroll to Hoan Kiem lake: a beautiful, expansive body of water right in the center of this bustling city. I cross the street and zigzag around parked motorbikes and people crouching peeling vegetables, changing bike oil, smoking, and tipping half-eaten bowls of noodles into buckets in the gutter. Weaving through the Old Quarter and into the shoe-selling district, and under the cover of trees alongside the water's edge.

I have no desire to be anywhere else. I just sit beneath a tree, in the shade, observing and listening to the world. There's so much to take in. A group of old women practice t'ai chi, egg and pork bánh mì baguettes are sold from baskets, birds glide, just breaking the water's surface with their claws. The whole city carefully controls their every movement, the slowness and precision of each breath, being completely present in every moment.

I'm continuously met with the smiling, friendly local faces who jump at the chance to practice their English with me. It's amazing how despite our differences in backgrounds, the topic of creating a meaningful life always resonates. The atmosphere here is one built upon the strength of community. Togetherness. There is no hustling based on fake appearance. Or artificial conversations. There's a realness that I'd never encountered anywhere else before.

I stroll the tree-lined boulevards, watching the world unfold in front of me. The roads thrive with life, carrying commerce the way a vein moves blood. Everyone here follows their passion. They all have a craft and skill which they hone and perfect. Women in conical hats sit in open-air markets and sell the freshest dried shrimp, rice, natural medicines, vegetables, eels, and flowers. Grand canvases with ornate imagery of Vietnam hang in shop fronts while the local metal workers tinker and fix the many motorbikes, to the baristas who blend the best coffee. They focus their time, energy, and effort into what they love. And it shows.

The narrow roads are a hive of activity. They brim with countless motor scooters, trucks, and carts with an inviting collection of fresh fruits piled precariously high. Most of the roads are lined with stalls—rusty shelters that sold axles, bricks, food, lampposts, refrigerators, and everything else the mind can conceive. The weather is damp and hot, like a curtain, and infused with smoke from barbecues cooking on the pavements, petrol fumes, and exotic spices.

Every afternoon the Reunification Express weaves its path between the narrow streets, tightly squeezing between the narrow alleys with coffee shops on either side with tourists gazing at the sight. Then across the center of Long Bien Bridge with its bold and distinct copper-red structure standing out from the luscious green scenery on either side before disappearing into the distance. The daily passing of the train reminds me time is always moving and I have to make the most of my time on Earth and appreciate all the seemingly insignificant moments within each day.

While simply wandering the streets, observing the day extend out in front of me, it became more obvious to me than ever before my dream life exists only in the journey. I wasn't aiming at a milestone or goal anymore. Instead, I want this life to last an eternity. No longer am I rushing for bigger, faster, better. I am savoring, soaking in the atmosphere, and enjoying everything that comes my way.

I still face difficulties, challenges, and struggles, but as opposed to these being stress-inducing and mental health-destroying like they once were in the corporate world, they feel meaningful. It's a sign I am still striving forward but in a way that improves myself and the world. Previously I put up with the hardships for the bigger goal, the next hit of dopamine and approval, all in the aim of more money, power, and status to boost my ego. Not anymore.

Now I know I am really pursuing my dream, working on my real ambitions and staying true to myself. While I am moving toward a more positive, better place, I also realize in the very act of moving, this is my dream life in action. The motion, progress, challenges, mishaps, celebrations, and misunderstandings are all an important part of my journey. I can't rush something that I want to last forever.

Some afternoons, I saunter, taking myself off to a deserted rooftop and just looking over the sprawling city. It's beautiful. Twenty stories below, the pulse of the city drifts up, as if resembling the sounds and sights of a carnival. I can see the neon signs flicker, headlights of countless motor scooters illuminate French-colonial buildings and treelined boulevards, balcony's full of exotic plants, the occasional patch of smoke wisping in the air, and the rumble of the train. Observing the city from here was like listening to a well-orchestrated symphony.

I've obtained the heights I wanted, just not how I thought. The glass box at the top of the shining building was not important. Looking at the view over Hanoi, stretching into the distance, with the energy that glows from the very people, I am reminded how much desperation was inside of me to reach the top. How badly I wanted the view. How desperately I wanted the distance between me and the ground to be endless miles apart. I like being here, hidden from view, watching life. It shows me how the longing for heights was a distraction from being comfortable with who I was. Who I always have been.

As the evening draws in, I seek out a street food spot for dinner. I sit on a small plastic stall on the pavement, amongst the locals as the exciting rush of the city continues beside me. The food is deep with flavor and has a freshness I've never tasted before and as the local beer hits the back of my throat, I feel refreshed. There are no fancy waiters, no champagne flutes, no red carpet on arrival, no small talk. It's just authentic and humble living.

After I take the last mouthful, carefully moving the chopsticks toward my lips, I savor the moment. Taking in a deep breath, I feel the humidity slightly stick my t-shirt to my chest, the motorbikes maneuver on the road next to me, the chatter amongst the locals. Life is a series of moments, and they are all we really ever have. There is no big finale. No firework display to come. Just this moment. Here. Right now.

I took what are considered large risks to get here. I had to leave what was considered the pinnacle of my career. I departed from the fast-lane lifestyle. I decided to leave behind my old ambitions. But the biggest risk of all would have been not pursuing what I knew was my true calling. The most monumental mistake would have been not to follow that voice whispering deep within. That calls in the night. That murmurs on your breath. That fills your heart with warmth.

As I grow older with each day, the more I accept the truth that life is short. I have to focus on what I want. Finally. And believe in that whole-heartedly. When you start listening to that voice and following the path it lays out in front of you, it's amazing how quickly and positively things unfold.

Opportunities start opening, amazing friendships are created, profound conversations are created, exciting projects start materializing. As I sit and stare into the world, this feeling inside speaks to me that says, *I have to do this. I know this is right.*

I'm privileged to have experienced everything in my journey so far. They were lessons that were teaching me, and I needed to make the most of that opportunity. And do something good with it. My perspective has shifted forever. There is no going back. I always trusted everyone around me knew what was best for me. Now I trust myself. I've built a stronger relationship with who I am and what I want from life. Formed from my own truths, experiences, and knowledge; not opinions, other's preferences, and societal norms.

My mind occasionally flashes back to the evenings craving tiny white pills, the emptiness I felt when scrolling on my phone late at night, the mental sacrifices of relentlessly climbing. I almost shudder. It's been difficult to process. But I remind myself of how lucky I have really been—to have discovered these truths early on. To have resisted. To have made it out the other side, better.

As the sun fades to darkness, I gaze up at the sky, so dense with stars that the black net of night appears as if it is overflowing with a glittering haul. Walking back through the streets, weaving between motorbikes, hearing the sound of local instruments lift from the street, children playing in the alleyways, a stray dog meandering, I realize Vietnam is also teaching me. To find the things I want to chase, create values that are intrinsically meaningful; but most of all exploring

the peace and space I once had, on those late summer evenings, running freely playing football, with no expectations
of what I should be doing.

Later, I lay back in a comfortable darkness, under the carelessly revolving ceiling fan. The white ceiling above stares
back at me. Beneath, the street that had been packed in
daylight is muffled and subdued. As I lay, images of memories from my time in Hanoi tumble and turn in my mind,
and my blood is so full of hope and possibility that I can't
help but smile.

I reflect on how different my life is. Being here, on the other
side of the world. I'm miles from the past but even further
from my old dreams with the glass corner office, the huge
team, and Ferrari parked outside. That was the old me. Not
only has my lifestyle changed, but so have my beliefs and
values. I am a different person. I am the real me. And I am
free. In ways I had always been free. But now I was free from
my own mind, free from my old beliefs. Free to live. Most
importantly, free to be myself.

CHAPTER 11:

Reflections

"Often people attempt to live their lives backwards: they try to have more things, or more money, in order to do more of what they want so that they will be happier. The way it actually works is the reverse. You first must be who you really are, then do what you really need to do, in order to have what you want."

—MARGARET YOUNG

When I was a child, I thought I was certain and definite on my ideas about life. I was asked so many times what I wanted to be when I grew up, so I made seeking the answer my primary pursuit. Deep within, deeper than I ever knew, I had the burning desire to grow up and be somebody. I came to believe this was the point of my life. But it was in fact a programming.

Cultural pressures were strong and so the messages priming me to conform and fit in clouded my mind. The system, with the heavy advertising, the worship of work as a moral virtue, the propagandizing forcing you to spend and work more, had distracted me from the truth of life. So I was left with an indescribable sense of dissatisfaction. It had become an internalized oppression.

From playground antics about fashion senses and hairstyles to enjoying popular music, I was told to blindly follow the crowd and to never question it. But I began to shape my ideas about life as extensions from these superficial external comments. I spent years chasing a life that was as a result of predetermined ambitions, instructed to pursue money at all costs, told to fit in regardless of the price I would have to pay: this was a trapped way of living.

I thought that diligently progressing through the education system followed by a thriving career, forever climbing up the ladder, was the right choice. Because that was all I was ever told. And I longed to be like my favorite business tycoons, Hollywood actors, Instagram influencers with their star-studded, glamorous, success-soaked paths.

I had given in to society's constantly changing and ever-increasing mandate expecting me to be so much: career and financial success, material possessions, physical health and fitness, social status. From pushing yourself out of your comfort zone, climbing the mystical ladder, demonstrating perfect relationships and perfect behaviors at all times no matter the sacrifice, all while living in a mentally stable, clear mind. And I had fallen into the dangerously imposed toxic level of obsessive perfectionism, accomplishment-seeking, and validation-hunting.

But the cost of this addictive prescription was who I was. The way I had been taught to live almost killed me.

I was living the magical dream everyone told me I should have aimed for. Mission accomplished, I thought. It impressed people and I gripped onto this fleeting, temporary feeling of validation that I longed for. But I was back at square one as it didn't make me feel secure in myself. I thought that constantly climbing, earning, and pursuing would give me bulletproof satisfaction. But that day never came.

I had unknowingly signed myself up for a hamster wheel existence where nothing was ever enough. A reality of mindless sleepwalking. It was an anti-climax waiting to happen, a lack of purpose that soon became too intense to keep ignoring.

The day I really achieved my goal was when I gave it all up. When I felt like I no longer needed the fancy job title, fast car, and nods of approval. When I was secure enough in myself. Only now I realize, that was the goal I was trying to achieve all along.

To discover this, I had journeyed into the dark void of constantly desiring more, never feeling enough, greed, excess, indulgence, selfishness, all in the name of success, and it took me many years to finally see the illusion of it all. But now I am through the other side.

All the difficulty I had imagined had been artificially constructed in my mind. So much of my life had been lived in the constant fear of what may happen when my fairytale, externally-perfect life shattered. If I could ever live with the idea of not being the persistently strong, high-achieving, continually climbing and striving person.

I had been conditioned not only to perpetually live in this constant façade but to profess that I, in fact, desired it.

However, if I hadn't had my experiences with the mental battles I faced, the dark and lonely days, my life may have been easier. I may have been viewed as more successful, had more money, appeared to have a better life. It may have seemed better, but I would have been less. The challenges, conflicts, doubt, and anxiety, made me who I am today; have become a part of me. It's who I am.

Now having sought the truth, everything has changed. Everything apart from my essence. I thought that by transforming, I would lose who I was. My mind being slowly re-formed. My body growing into its new shape. But I didn't alter my image, I discovered it. I didn't change my mind. I opened it.

I wondered whether my start would also be my end. Whether I would stay constant. If my old version of myself was my only true shape. I realized I am not fixed. I can evolve. And now I have.

I hear the ongoing issues riddled in the world I once knew and was a part of. The intensity, the stress, the unhealthiness of it all. But thankfully these voices are in the distance to me now. Maybe one day I will return, whether I will be permanently separated or if one day I will find a way back. But I know that this new life has brought me peace.

This clarity did not come easily. I spent years justifying my choices, sacrificing the pursuit of the modern dream, desperately putting trust in myself even though at times I doubted who I was. But I eventually was able to cut this from my life. To catch my breath at last.

Although there are moments that have brought extreme clarity to my situation. I don't think there is one moment that resulted in my new beliefs, in me changing. But for years I felt a voice deep within myself whispering back to me. I was cracking and splintering from what I was supposed to be doing. And now I have broken free.

Through a desperate need to make a big change in my life, I learned to take the shackles off that prevented me from being who I truly was. And spending my life becoming my own person, becoming who I really am. The closer I have got to who I am, expressing myself in the way I want, with the words I want to, the happier I have become. The less I fit in, the less I conform to the misguided beliefs around me. The more I discover my own ambitions instead of ones I was imprisoned by, the better my life has been.

Everything that's important will accept this new version. Because it's not actually different. It is the version of myself underneath the performance. Behind the created and crafted appearance I had formed. I have never been purer. There are no other versions anymore. This is me.

I want to be me. To think for myself. To be myself. We shouldn't aspire to be more like our idols, we should be aspiring to be even more like ourselves. The unfiltered, uncaring, unassuming, intrinsically motivated version of ourselves.

Maybe that is the whole point of life—we are on the never-ending journey to being ourselves.

A transformation, maybe. A journey in becoming who I really am. I call it breaking free.

Acknowledgments

Thank you to my financial backers who made this book possible: Aaron Wilson, James Lo, Matthew Spencer, Amy Dykes, Joe Andrews, Jake Clarke, Thomas Heywood, Lauren Windebank, Joe Briody, Matthew Phelan, Flynn Blackie, Amida Adamu, Haroon Perveez, Karishma Vyas, Albert Edwards, Neale Powell-Cook, Stephen Briody, Kevin McCumiskey, Thomas Truckle, Georgina Moat, Jack Nolan, Hector Hughes, Haider Ali, Terrence Sear, Susie Hill-Smith, Heidi Davis, Daniel Boles, Margaret Curran, Libby Simms, James Goforth, Ruby Swan, Moria Dopson, Mary Drysdale, Kathae Brown, Rita and Don Swain.

Thank you to my early readers for their excellent feedback: Jennie Dalton, Albert Edwards, Joe Briody, Susie Hill-Smith, Richard Marks, Georgina Moat, Claire Swan, Syrie Bibby.

Thank you to my parents for all their support on my book journey. My wonderful editors Collen Young and Alan Zatkow for their dedication and hard work and for helping me turn my vision for the book into reality. To Eric Koester for believing in my book right from the start. To the team at New Degree Press for all their work behind the scenes in making this book possible. Thank you to Steven Bartlett for inspiring me along the way.

Appendix

CHAPTER 6: THE ONE MINUTE I REALIZED EVERYTHING.
Murakami, Haruki. *Kafka on the Shore*. London: Harvill, 2005.